champions
of the ring

T H E   G R E A T   F I G H T E R S

champions
of the ring

THE GREAT FIGHTERS

Illustrated biographies
of the biggest names
in boxing history

AUTHOR **PETER BROOKE-BALL**

CONTRIBUTING EDITORS **DEREK O'DELL** AND **O. F. SNELLING**

southwater

This edition is published by Southwater

Distributed in the UK by
The Manning Partnership
251–253 London Road East
Batheaston
Bath BA1 7RL
tel. 01225 852 727
fax 01225 852 852

Published in the USA by
Anness Publishing Inc.
27 West 20th Street
Suite 504
New York
NY 10011
fax 212 807 6813

Distributed in Canada by
General Publishing
895 Don Mills Road
400–402 Park Centre
Toronto, Ontario M3C 1W3
tel. 416 445 3333
fax 416 445 5991

Distributed in Australia by
Sandstone Publishing
Unit 1, 360 Norton Street
Leichhardt
New South Wales 2040
tel. 02 9560 7888
fax 02 9560 7488

ILLUSTRATIONS
Page 1: *(Left)* Pinklon Thomas v Trevor
Berbick; *(Right)* James 'Quick' Tillis
v Frank Bruno
Page 2: Thomas Hearns v 'Sugar' Ray
Leonard
Page 3: Willie Pep *(seen here on the right)*
v Ray Farnechon
Page 4: *(Right)* James 'Quick' Tillis
v Frank Bruno; *(Left)* Roberto Duran
(seen here on the left) v Ken Buchanon
Page 5: John Mugabi v Marvin Hagler

Southwater is an imprint of Anness Publishing Limited
Hermes House, 88–89 Blackfriars Road, London SE1 8HA
tel. 020 7401 2077; fax 020 7633 9499

© Anness Publishing Limited 2001

Publisher Joanna Lorenz
Managing Editor Judith Simons
Project Editors Sarah Ainley, Felicity Forster and Johnnie Glasses
Art Director Peter Bridgewater
Designers Peter Laws and Axis Design
Jacket design Bridgewater
Production Controller Yolande Denny

Previously published as part of a larger volume, *Boxing*.
1 3 5 7 9 10 8 6 4 2

ACKNOWLEDGEMENTS
The majority of the photographs in this volume are from the private collections of O. F. Snelling and Derek O'Dell.
Additional material has been supplied by their many friends in the world of boxing, and is used with their approval.
Mr Snelling wishes particularly to thank R. A. Hartley, bookseller and boxing bibliographer; Harry Mullan, editor of *Boxing News*;
Mrs Ethal Crome, widow of the late Tom Crome; Mr and Mrs Peter McInnes, dealers in boxing books and ephemera; and Charles Taylor.
Mr O'Dell would like to express his special thanks to David Allen, boxing collector; George Zeleny and the staff of Boxing Outlook; and David Roake.
The publishers extend grateful thanks to AllSport, Popperfoto and Sporting Pictures for supplying many of the colour photographs of
fights and boxers of the modern era. The publishers have attempted where relevant and where possible to trace the original sources
of archive and other materials used in the book, and to seek permissions and offer acknowledgements where appropriate.
They apologize for any omissions, oversights, or occasions when efforts to make contact or trace sources have proved fruitless.
The publishers would be pleased to hear from any uncontacted sources so that these acknowledgements may be updated for future editions.

★
CONTENTS

INTRODUCTION
6

THE
BARE-KNUCKLE
CHAMPIONS
8

CHAMPIONS OF
THE GLOVED ERA
24

INDEX
128

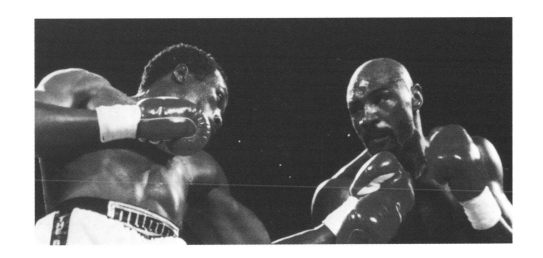

INTRODUCTION

Each era produces its great boxing champions. A selection of the all-time favourites – those who were, or are, household names – are shown here in all their championship glory.

Inevitably, readers will be tempted to make comparisons: would Joe Louis have out-punched Jack Dempsey or could Mike Tyson have done the same to Muhammad Ali? How would a prime Benny Leonard have fared against Roberto Duran of the late 1970s? Some feel that the old-timers were superior to today's stars, while others feel that the reverse is the case.

No myths – and there are plenty of them – have been perpetuated in these biographical sketches. We trace each boxer's career from often tenuous beginnings and then highlight his championship achievements. Of all the thousands of men who have climbed through the ropes since the Marquess of Queensberry rules were introduced, only a few have stamped their names indelibly in the annals of fistic history. Some kept their money and lived out their remaining years in comfort. Others fell by the wayside and sank into obscurity, but they were all masters of their craft inside the ring, and in the pages that follow, that is how they are remembered.

Left: Jeff Harding is carried aloft after taking the WBC light-heavyweight title from the holder Dennis Andries on June 24 1989 in Atlantic City. Andries reclaimed the title from the Australian the following year with a knockout win.

Left: The rivalry between Ezzard Charles (right) and 'Jersey' Joe Walcott was one of the fiercest in boxing history. The pair fought for the world heavyweight crown four times. Charles won on the first two occasions, but Walcott took the title in July 1951 (seen here), and he defended it in June 1952.

THE BARE-KNUCKLE CHAMPIONS

On these two pages are shown a host of champions and nearly-men from the 1890s and 1900s – the golden age of the fight game, when bare-fisted sluggers gave way to the modern giants. Smaller pictures: top rank, left to right: Jim Fell; Joe McAuliffe; Frank Craig; Mike Donovan; 'Denver' Ed Smith. Middle rank: Jim Daly; Joe Goss; Jack Welch; Jack Ashton; John Donaldson. Bottom rank: Samuel Blakelock; Captain J C Dailey; William Sheriff; Frank Herald; 'Sparrow' Golden. Above left: Jimmy Carney. Above right: George Godfrey. Right: Jimmy Carroll.

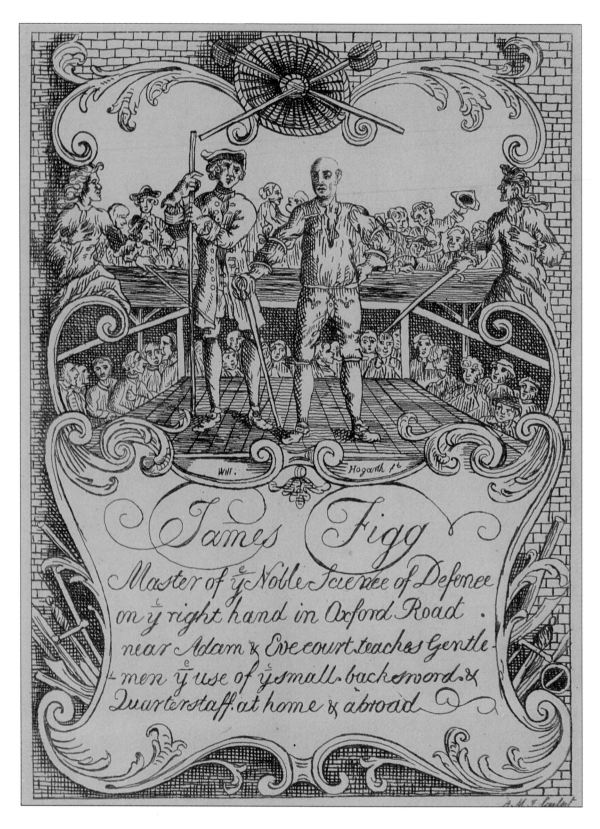

Above: James Figg's card of 1719, which was engraved for him by his friend, the great English painter William Hogarth. This was the first advertisement for the 'Noble Science of Defence'. In addition to boxing, Figg also taught his clients how to use the sword and the quarterstaff.

Right: John (Jack) Broughton (1704–1789) is regarded as the 'Father of Boxing'. He established a boxing school and arena near the Haymarket in London, and he encouraged his pupils to wear gloves so that they would not inflict too much damage on each other. After one of his defeated opponents, George Stevenson, died, Broughton introduced a set of rules which remained in force for the best part of a century. He became a Yeoman of the Guard at the Tower of London and there is a memorial to him in Westminster Abbey.

THE EARLY CHAMPIONS

An Oxfordshire-born Englishman by the name of James Figg is credited with the rebirth of boxing, when, in 1719, he advertised a boxing exhibition at his booth at Southwark Fair in London. Figg was better known at the time as a cudgel-fighter and swordsman but he nevertheless claimed to be boxing's first champion and he went on to open his celebrated amphitheatre off the Tottenham Court Road in what is now the West End of London. One of Figg's major achievements was to attract the attention of England's gentry. He was lucky enough to be a close friend of the painter William Hogarth who not only completed a portrait of the fighter but also produced illustrated publicity leaflets for him. So, as well as being the first champion, Figg also became the first promoter, not just for himself but for everyone involved.

Figg had many fistic encounters at his amphitheatre, where the arena was surrounded by wooden planks, and he even attracted international opposition. One of his most famous fights was against a Venetian gondolier who nearly got the better of Figg before eventually being flattened by a body blow. Figg retired undefeated in 1734 and one of his pupils, George Taylor, assumed the title of champion. In 1740 Taylor was beaten by Jack Broughton, who immediately began to revolutionize the art of boxing. Three years after beating Taylor, Broughton built his own amphitheatre, complete with a raised stage, in Hanway Street and drafted a set of rules which transformed the sport. Until Broughton's Rules were published, there were virtually no codes of conduct and a boxer was consequently allowed to use any tactic he wished.

Broughton remained champion until 1750 when he was beaten by Jack Slack, a Norwich butcher, who

Right: Daniel Mendoza (1763–1836) was a clever man and the most skilful boxer of his era. He managed his own affairs and is thought to be the first person to introduce a 'gate' at which spectators had to pay in order to see a contest. The first Jewish champion, he introduced new defensive techniques to boxing and he had a great influence on subsequent generations of fighters.

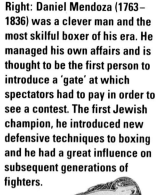

Above: John Smith, called 'Buckhorse', was a familiar figure in the London rings during the middle of the eighteenth century. His ugliness was only in part due to bare-knuckle fighting as he was born with a misshapen face. He had a reputation for being an outstandingly brave and powerful fighter.

MENDOZA.

became known as the 'Knight of the Cleaver'. However Broughton was hailed as the 'Father of Boxing' and during his reign he was much favoured by the aristocracy, especially the Duke of Cumberland. In fact he was so adored by men from all walks of life that when he died at the age of eighty-five a special memorial stone was laid for him in no less a place than Westminster Abbey.

Jack Slack and his contemporaries did little for boxing and the sport lost favour and reputation, not only with the public, but with wealthy patrons as well. Slack himself was at first seen to be a brave and able fighter; but he later resorted to using unfair, open-fisted 'chops' and he frequently bribed opponents to lose. He was not averse to taking bribes himself and when he lost the title to Bill 'The Nailer' Stevens in

1760, his backer, the powerful Duke of Cumberland, suspecting that he had accepted payment, turned his back on boxing for good. Equally disillusioned, the public shunned fights while the boxers determined the championship among themselves based on who could pay the biggest bribes.

A new era of bare-knuckle fighting began with the arrival on the pugilist scene of a Spanish-English Jew by the name of Daniel Mendoza who became so famous when he beat Sam 'Butcher' Martin in 1787 that he pronounced himself champion. However it was not until he had got the better of Bill Warr in seventeen minutes on Bexley Heath in 1794 that he was universally acknowledged as undisputed champion of England. Mendoza was unusually intelligent for a boxer of the time, and he cultivated the art of

Right: 'Gentleman' John Jackson (1769–1845) was a canny boxer and was given his nickname because of his good manners and dandy's clothes. However when he wrested the championship from Mendoza in 1795, he is supposed to have held his opponent's head by the hair as he punched him into oblivion. Jackson had friends in high places and taught Lord Byron, among others, to box at his school in Old Bond Street, London.

Above: Richard Humphries beat Daniel Mendoza twice, in 1787 and 1788, before the latter became champion. However Mendoza avenged those defeats in 1789 and 1790, and, after the fourth fight, Humphries decided that he had had enough and retired.

defence which had largely been ignored in favour of developing strength and endurance. Mendoza's tactics were admired by many but not by all; some, unused to this new and artful style, proclaimed him a coward as he cannily moved around the ring to gain an advantage. Mendoza's strategy was, however, adopted by a new generation of boxers, most particularly in Ireland, which he toured and where he eventually established a boxing school. Mendoza lost his crown to 'Gentleman' John Jackson in 1795 (in what was by every account a not very gentlemanly fight) and retired to write his *Memoirs*. He returned to the ring eleven years later, aged fifty-seven, but gave up for good after losing to Tom Owen.

Like Mendoza, 'Gentleman' John Jackson, so-called because he dressed in dandy's clothes and was

Above: 'Jem' Belcher (1781–1811) beat many of the best boxers of his day but ironically is most remembered for the fights he lost – especially those against Tom Cribb. Called the 'Napoleon of the Ring' because of his clever strategies, he lost an eye while playing rackets in 1803 and relinquished his title to Henry 'Game Chicken' Pearce in 1805. He is thought to have been the first person to place his 'colours' on the corner post of a ring.

Right: Thomas Cribb (1781–1848) was a comparatively slow boxer but sturdy and determined for all that. His greatest bouts were against Tom Molineaux whom he fought twice, in 1810 and 1811, winning both times. He retired to run a public house and such was his popularity that when he died a memorial was erected to him by public subscription in Woolwich Churchyard.

well-spoken, was a 'scientific' boxer who heavily relied on nimble footwork for his victories. Like several champions before him he ran a boxing school; it was situated at no. 13 Old Bond Street, London, and among his pupils was Lord Byron who dubbed him the 'Emperor of Pugilism'.

One of the most well-liked and respected boxers at the turn of the century was John ('Jem') Belcher who was the grandson of Jack Slack, the infamous former champion. He reigned supreme from 1800 to 1803 when he lost an eye while playing rackets. He retired for a time but came back two years later and fought Henry Pearce who beat him in thirteen rounds. He boxed two more contests, both against Tom Cribb, but lost on each occasion and eighteen months later died at the tender age of thirty.

One of the most extraordinary characters ever to box was John Gully, who came from a well-to-do family but had been thrown into a debtors' prison as a result of a business venture that failed. In those days there was little hope of ever getting out of a debtors' jail, but Gully had earned a reputation as a competent amateur fighter and the reigning champion, Henry Pearce, entered the prison to spar with him. Gully, by all accounts, got the better of the champion and the news spread far and wide. In due course, Gully's debts were paid by a benevolent sportsman on the condition that he would fight Pearce for the championship of England.

The two met on October 8 1805 at Hailsham in Sussex. After sixty-four rounds Gully was beaten, but not before putting up an impressive show. So much so that when Pearce retired he declared Gully to be his successor. Not everybody was satisfied with this conclusion, so Gully was obliged to fight the 'Lancashire Giant', Bob Gregson. After Gregson had

Right: The first fight between 'Jem' Belcher and Tom Cribb at Moulsey Hurst on April 8 1807. Belcher had the better of the fight, but had to retire with shattered hands. 'What did I tell you?', cried a bloody Cribb as Belcher left, unable to throw another punch: 'I said that my head would break his hands to pieces!'

Below: The magnificent early champion, Henry 'Game Chicken' Pearce.

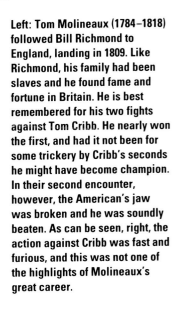

HEN° PEARCE

FROM AN OLD ENGRAVING.

Left: Tom Molineaux (1784–1818) followed Bill Richmond to England, landing in 1809. Like Richmond, his family had been slaves and he found fame and fortune in Britain. He is best remembered for his two fights against Tom Cribb. He nearly won the first, and had it not been for some trickery by Cribb's seconds he might have become champion. In their second encounter, however, the American's jaw was broken and he was soundly beaten. As can be seen, right, the action against Cribb was fast and furious, and this was not one of the highlights of Molineaux's great career.

SHUREY'S EDITION. ONE PENNY.

FAMOUS FIGHTS

PAST AND PRESENT. EDITED BY HAROLD FURNISS

Vol. III.—No. 31. TOM CRIBB'S SECOND BATTLE WITH MOLINEAUX.

Above: James ('Jem') Ward was a distinguished boxer, but his character was more dubious. His reign as champion came during a period when boxing was part of the underworld, and notorious for 'fixes' and out-of-ring violence. He was the first champion ever to regain his crown, when he beat Simon Byrne in 1831.

Right: Irishman Simon Byrne, 'The Emerald Gem', shows his class against Phillip Sampson, 'The Birmingham Youth', in 1829. Sampson was no match for Byrne, and despite being physically carried to the scratch by his seconds on numerous occasions, he eventually gave way to the slaughter after one hundred and four minutes.

been soundly beaten twice, in 1807 and 1808, Gully was acknowledged as the genuine champion; but after the second contest he vowed that he would never fight in the ring again. Among those who pleaded with him to change his mind was the Duke of York, but Gully's resolution stayed firm and he went on to amass a great fortune. He established a racing stable and two of his horses won the Derby. He also acquired land and coal mines and in 1832 was elected a Member of Parliament. He died a wealthy and successful man in 1863 at the age of eighty.

After Gully had retired in 1808 Tom Cribb laid claim to the crown and challenged the one-eyed 'Jem' Belcher for the championship in their second encounter. He won the contest in thirty-one rounds in 1809 and successfully defended his title in two epic encounters against the black American, Tom Molineaux. Cribb did not fight professionally again after his second bout with Molineaux in 1811, but continued to hold the title until 1822, when he named Tom Spring as his successor.

Spring proved to be a worthy champion and remained undefeated upon his retirement in 1824 after two classic fights against the Irish champion, Jack Langan. Tom Cannon claimed the title after Spring, but his reign was short-lived and he was beaten by 'Jem' Ward in 1825. Ward was a shady character and is known to have bet money on himself to lose. However he became the first man to regain the championship title after losing it. He was defeated by Peter 'Young Rump Steak' Crawley in 1827, but became champion again four years later when he beat the Irishman, Simon Byrne. In 1831 Ward was presented with a Championship Belt, the first awarded.

Above: James 'Deaf 'Un' Burke was born in 1809 and died in 1845. He was well-liked, though a rogue of the first water. He was a successful fighter, and worked his way up to become champion in 1833. In that year he had his most famous fight – one of the most brutal recorded in the history of the sport. He fought Simon Byrne at a place called No-Man's-Land in Hertfordshire, and the two men went at it for ninety-nine rounds which lasted one hundred and eighty-six minutes: Byrne died two days later of his injuries.

THE FIGHT BETWEEN DEAF BURKE AND BILL FITZMAURICE.

Vol. II.—No. 21.

James Burke, known as the 'Deaf 'Un', called himself champion after Ward's retirement but Simon Byrne disputed his claim. To settle the issue, Burke and Byrne fought a bitter battle in 1833 that lasted three hours, six minutes for a total of ninety-nine rounds. Burke won the undisputed title, while the unfortunate Byrne was carried off, and died of his injuries soon after. Burke was forced to flee to America because of the ensuing furore and there he fought an old enemy, Samuel O'Rourke, in New Orleans. O'Rourke was a mobster and hoodlum and

Above: Burke in action against Bill Fitzmaurice. Burke eventually triumphed after one hundred and sixty-six rounds which lasted two minutes under three hours. Fitzmaurice may have been hampered in his challenge by the absence of his manager, Charlie Gibletts, who was in prison at the time, having been caught body-snatching in Bishop's Stortford.

Left: The fight between Ben Caunt and John Leechman, 'Brassey of Bradford', on October 26 1840 at Six Mile Bottom, between Newmarket and Cambridge. The fight was attended by many of the sporting nobility, including the Duke of Beaufort, the Marquis of Worcester, the Marquis of Exeter, and Lord George Bentinck: it was just as well that a group of special constables sent to hunt out and stop the battle were guilefully diverted to another county. Caunt downed his man for good in the one-hundredth round.

Above: William Abednego Thompson, called 'Bendigo' in fight circles, was one of the most remarkable ring characters of these early days. In this fight he beat 'Young' Langan in one hour thirty-three minutes, after spending most of the preliminary stages shamming that he was too hurt to continue. Langan relaxed in anticipation of victory, and, with his defences down, 'Bendigo' was able to land a winning blow. He proceeded to take the championship from Caunt shortly afterwards.

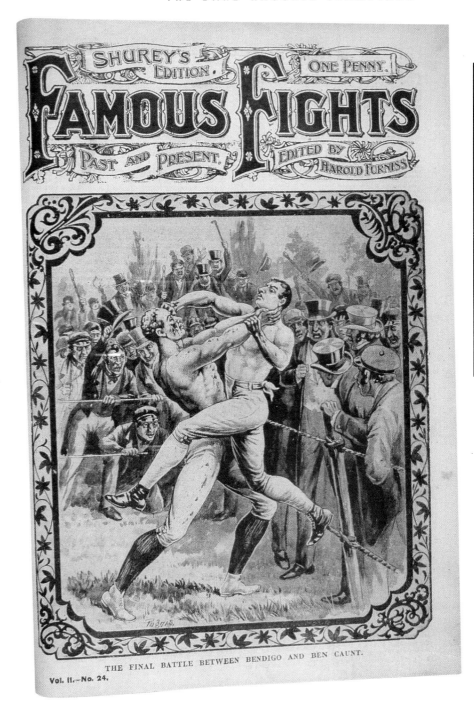

SHUREY'S EDITION. ONE PENNY.

FAMOUS FIGHTS

PAST AND PRESENT. EDITED BY HAROLD FURNISS

THE FINAL BATTLE BETWEEN BENDIGO AND BEN CAUNT.

Vol. II.—No. 24.

Above and left: William 'Bendigo' Thompson (1811–1880) was a fiery character who was in perpetual trouble with the law. He first won the championship from Ben Caunt in 1835, then lost it to the same man in 1838. 'Bendigo' got the better of James Burke in 1839, and regained the championship title in a third bloody battle against Caunt in 1845. In later years 'Bendigo' gave up his former ways and became a preacher. The town of Bendigo in Australia is named after him and a play has been written about his extraordinary life. The scene, left, is from 'Bendigo's' last fight against Caunt.

his cronies broke up the fight in the third round when they saw that their boss was losing. Burke escaped and went to New York where he had one fight before returning to England. In 1839, Burke fought William 'Bendigo' Thompson (a fighter who had won and lost the championship title in the intervening years), but was disqualified for head-butting.

Thompson was a curious man. He was one of triplets who were nicknamed Shadrach, Meshach and Abednego, the last being corrupted to 'Bendigo'. Short and stocky, he was not the cleanest of fighters but he was nevertheless brave and resourceful. Before beating Burke, he had had two notorious en-

counters with Ben Caunt for the championship, and each man had won one contest when the other was disqualified for fouling. When they met for the third time, in 1845, a ferocious struggle took place with both men employing nasty tactics. 'Bendigo' eventually got the better of his old adversary in ninety-three rounds after Caunt broke the rules by going down without being struck. 'Bendigo's' last fight was in 1850 against Tom Paddock, who was disqualified when he struck the champion while he was down. 'Bendigo' retired after his fight with Paddock and during one of his frequent later spells in prison he had a mystical revelation. He consequently became an evangelist and travelled the world preaching.

Right: Tom Sayers (1826–1865) is one of the most famous of all bare-knuckle fighters. Small and light, he was only ever beaten once, by Nat Langham. His 1860 fight against the American, John C Heenan, ranks among the greatest of all time, despite the fact that it ended in a draw. Nicknamed 'Peerless' because of his skill, he was buried at London's famous Highgate cemetery.

Above: Bill Richmond (1763–1829) was the son of an American slave who learned his boxing skills while sparring against British soldiers stationed in the United States. He was brought to England by the Duke of Northumberland and had several impressive victories before being knocked out by Tom Cribb. He was the first black boxer to rise to prominence and he continued to fight until he was fifty-six, at which age he knocked out Jack Carter.

THE FIRST CHAMPIONS IN THE UNITED STATES

By the middle of the nineteenth century, boxing had taken root in America. Many English and Irish fighters had toured the country giving exhibition bouts, and several Americans, most notably the ex-slaves Bill Richmond and Tom Molineaux, had come to fight in England. A New Yorker by the name of Jacob Hyer is considered the 'Father of the American Ring'. He was the first American to fight professionally and his match against Tom Beasley in 1816 was the first to be fought to British Prize Ring Rules. In 1849 Hyer's son, Tom, became the first heavyweight champion of America when he beat 'Yankee' Sullivan, an Irish émigré. After Tom Hyer retired, another Irish-American, John Morissey, beat 'Yankee' Sullivan and the up-and-coming John C Heenan to claim the American title. Then Morissey retired and Heenan had nobody to fight. A suggestion was put forward that he challenge the reigning British champion,

Tom Sayers, to determine who would be the undisputed champion of the world.

Sayers, a bricklayer by trade, had clinched the British title by knocking out Tom Paddock in 1858. He was a small man and weighed little more than 150 pounds, but by the time he met Heenan, the 'Benecia Boy', in 1860, he had a formidable reputation for beating men far larger than himself. His one defeat had been in 1853 at the hands of Nat Langham.

In one of the most memorable fights in boxing history, the first international contest for a world title ended in a draw. Sayers did not fight again, and on his retirement Heenan assumed the crown of world champion. The two, in fact, became close friends and when Heenan went to England in 1863 to fight Tom King, Sayers acted as his second. Heenan lost that contest and both he and King retired shortly afterwards.

Heenan next morning
FROM PHOTO.

Above, left, and bottom: John C Heenan (1833–1873) came over to England in 1860 to fight Tom Sayers to decide who would be champion of the world. The fight was called a draw after crowd interference, with Heenan having to break away through the mob (bottom), but Heenan had had the English hero on the ropes. To look at Heenan's face on the day after the fight (above), there is no doubt that Sayers scored some good hits, too. Perhaps surprisingly, Heenan and Sayers became friends and they later fought exhibition matches together. Heenan returned to England in 1863 and lost to Tom King. He never fought again.

Right: This engraving, which was originally reproduced in a newspaper of the time, illustrates the procession at Tom Sayers' funeral in 1865.

Above: Peter Jackson was a talented boxer who bridged two eras, fighting both with and without gloves. He started his career in 1882 while in Australia and travelled to America in 1888. John L Sullivan refused to fight him because of his colour, but he fought a closely-contested sixty-one-round draw with James J Corbett in 1891.

Right: Jackson fights Corbett on May 21 1891 at the California Athletic Club: the men are wearing gloves, and a new age has begun.

Left and below: 'Jem' Mace could lay claim to being the last of the great bare-knuckle fighters: after him came Sullivan, and a new generation. In a tribute to him, *Famous Fights* proclaimed: 'In his prime Mace was one of the finest-looking athletes, and *the* most finished boxer we ever saw in the Prize Ring. Indeed, we think it is not too much to say that amongst the Champions of England, of whom he was the last, there was not one superior to him in science or Ring-craft.' He is pictured, below, at his peak, on the cover of the magazine.

THE LATE NINETEENTH
CENTURY

With the passing of the great Sayers and Heenan, boxing fell into some disarray, especially in England where it began to lose favour with the public. This was due, in no small part, to the preachings of the influential clergy who were united in their battle against fist-fighting. Jem Mace, who had once beaten Tom King, was acclaimed as the world champion but, like so many English boxers, he spent much of his time in the United States.

Mace's last fight, a draw, was against an American called Joe Coburn on November 30 1871. Coburn had laid claim to the American title in 1863 on beating another Irishman, Mike McCool. Five years later, however, McCool claimed the title when Coburn was arrested by the police just before their return bout was due to begin. An Englishman, Tom Allen, who had fled the victimization back in his own country, went on to defeat McCool in 1873. Joe Goss, another Englishman who had crossed the Atlantic, got the better of Allen in 1876, but lost to Paddy Ryan in an eighty-seven-round contest in 1880. Ryan's reign as American champion was brief and he got his come-uppance against no less a personage than the mighty John L Sullivan. With the coming of Sullivan was born a new breed of fighters, who were to become the first generation of the modern game.

CHAMPIONS OF THE GLOVED ERA

Above: The Cuban crowd goes wild in Havana on April 5 1915, as Jess Willard stands above the felled Jack Johnson. It is the twenty-sixth round of their heavyweight title bout, and Willard is about to don the crown he was to wear for the next four years.

Left: England's Frank Bruno is seen here when endeavouring, unsuccessfully, to wrest the heavyweight championship from Mike Tyson in 1989. Bruno finally won the WBC World title in 1994, only to have it snatched away by his old nemesis Mike Tyson early in 1996.

JOHN L SULLIVAN

John L Sullivan will forever be remembered as the first man to become officially recognized as the heavyweight champion of the world, although he claimed the title while boxing to Prize Ring Rules.

He was born of Irish parents in Boston, and as a teenager won a reputation for being something of a braggart, challenging all-comers to take him on and showing off his immense strength by lifting full beer barrels over his head. Not surprisingly, he was dubbed the 'Boston Strong Boy'.

Paddy Ryan, the reigning American champion, refused to fight Sullivan in 1880 so the 'Boston Strong Boy' went on a nation-wide tour, offering fifty dollars to anyone who could last four rounds with him in a ring (on a subsequent tour the challenge went up to $1,000 to anybody who could last four rounds). Nobody succeeded in taking money from him and in 1882 Ryan at last agreed to a fight. The contest took place at Mississippi City on February 7 1882, and Ryan was knocked out in nine rounds that lasted just under eleven minutes.

After his fight with Ryan, Sullivan claimed that he was both American and world champion but others disagreed, including Charlie Mitchell, the British champion. Mitchell and Sullivan first met in New York in 1883 and the Englishman went down in the third round. However, the fight never came to a completely satisfying conclusion, because the police burst in and broke it up. Another man left unhappy by Sullivan's claims was Jake Kilrain, who had challenged the 'Boston Strong Boy' to a contest but had been rejected. This refusal to fight prompted Richard K Fox, owner of the prestigious *Police Gazette*, to pronounce Kilrain champion. In 1887, outraged at Fox's impertinence, Boston businessmen clubbed together and gave Sullivan a $10,000 gold belt, inlaid with 397 diamonds, as

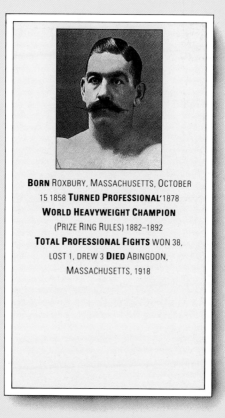

BORN ROXBURY, MASSACHUSETTS, OCTOBER 15 1858 **TURNED PROFESSIONAL** 1878 **WORLD HEAVYWEIGHT CHAMPION** (PRIZE RING RULES) 1882–1892 **TOTAL PROFESSIONAL FIGHTS** WON 38, LOST 1, DREW 3 **DIED** ABINGDON, MASSACHUSETTS, 1918

a token of the fact that, in their eyes, he was the genuine world champion.

A year after gaining his magnificent belt, Sullivan travelled to France where he encountered Mitchell for a second time. This bout lasted for thirty-nine rounds, but was abandoned as a draw because the foul weather made the conditions atrocious in the field where the ring was pitched. Sullivan was on top when the contest was stopped and the Englishman could count himself lucky that the weather came to his rescue.

After returning to the United States, Sullivan finally agreed to face Jake Kilrain. Their epic contest at Richburg, Mississippi, in 1889 lasted more than two hours before Kilrain succumbed in the seventy-fifth round. This was the last heavyweight contest to be fought under Prize Ring Rules and after it Sullivan claimed, with few arguments this time, that he was the undisputed world champion.

After the Kilrain contest Sullivan became something of a drunkard, but returned to the ring in 1892 to fight James J Corbett under Queensberry Rules in New Orleans. Hopelessly out of condition, Sullivan found himself out-boxed by the athletic young Californian and he was knocked out in twenty-one rounds.

Before his battle with Corbett, Sullivan had appeared in a play, *Honest Hearts and Willing Hands*, and he resumed his career on the stage afterwards, earning nearly $1 million by the time he retired in 1915. He also became a reformed character, and toured the land preaching against the evils of drink.

Sullivan steadfastly refused to fight black boxers throughout his career and thus avoided meeting the likes of Peter Jackson. Nevertheless, he became one of America's greatest and most fêted sporting heroes. He was never a subtle boxer but relied on brute strength and a formidable right hand to floor opponents.

Left: Sullivan is credited with creating the unified world heavyweight championship crown by eliminating all of the other contenders over a seven-year period. In 1882 he beat Paddy Ryan, the American champion; in 1883 he defeated Charlie Mitchell, champion of England; and in 1889 he finally met and fought the other great American pretender Kilrain (see below) in an epic encounter – the last bare-fist championship fight – which left Sullivan the undisputed king of the ring. He was 5 feet 10½ inches tall, and his top fighting weight was 190 pounds.

Above: Jake Kilrain, of Baltimore, was controversially declared champion of the world in 1887 when Sullivan refused a match with him. The two men eventually met on July 8 1889 to resolve the championship. After a seventy-five round bout that lasted two hours, sixteen minutes, and twenty-three seconds, Sullivan emerged the victor on a knock-out.

BOB FITZSIMMONS

Bob Fitzsimmons is dear to British hearts as he was the first English-born boxer to win the undisputed heavyweight championship of the world. When he was just nine years old, however, his Cornish parents emigrated to New Zealand and he was brought up in the town of Timaru, where his father set up in business as a blacksmith.

As soon as he was able, the young Fitzsimmons helped his father in the smithy, which is where he developed the massively impressive arm and chest muscles that were to prove so telling in later years. In 1880 the famous bare-knuckle fighter, 'Jem' Mace, travelled to New Zealand and organized a competition, which was duly won by the apprentice blacksmith. Mace recognized in Fitzsimmons a natural talent and encouraged him to take up a career as a professional.

Fitzsimmons furthered his boxing career in

BORN HELSTON, CORNWALL. DATE GIVEN VARIOUSLY AS JUNE 4 1862, JUNE 14 1862, MAY 26 1862, AND MAY 26 1863 **TURNED PROFESSIONAL** IN AUSTRALIA BETWEEN 1883–1888 **WORLD MIDDLEWEIGHT CHAMPION** 1891 **WORLD LIGHT-HEAVYWEIGHT CHAMPION** 1903–1905 **WORLD HEAVYWEIGHT CHAMPION** 1897–1899 **WORLD CHAMPIONSHIP FIGHTS** (HEAVYWEIGHT) WON 1, LOST 2; (MIDDLEWEIGHT) WON 2 (LIGHT-HEAVYWEIGHT) WON 1, LOST 1 **DIED** CHICAGO, OCTOBER 22 1917

Australia where he remained for ten years before setting sail for California in 1890. Fighting as a middleweight, he gained two quick successes in America before challenging Jack Dempsey, dubbed the 'Nonpareil' (because he was reckoned to be unbeatable), for the world title. The American pundits did not take the little-known Fitzsimmons seriously as a genuine contender. His torso and arms looked powerful enough, but his frail legs and receding hairline made him appear to be something of a joke. They were proved badly wrong when Fitzsimmons knocked out Dempsey in thirteen rounds.

After successfully defending his middleweight title against Dan Creedon in 1894, Fitzsimmons began to take on heavyweights whom he felled with remarkable regularity. After embracing American citizenship, he finally had a chance to challenge James J Corbett for the heavyweight crown in Carson City, Nevada, on

Right: Bob Fitzsimmons still rates as one of the most unlikely-looking fighters ever to have taken to the ring. He was 5 feet 11¾ inches tall, but weighed only 165 pounds: his legs could best be described as skinny, but the gangling form was topped by a stupendously strong torso, developed by years of working in his father's smithy. His weight allowed him to fight at middleweight, while his strength and courage made him more than a match for the heavier men of the day in the top division. He became the first boxer ever to win championships in three divisions when, towards the end of his career, he captured the newly-created light-heavyweight crown.

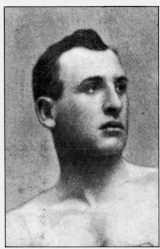

Above: Dan Creedon was born in New Zealand in 1868: he won the Australian middleweight championship before heading for America. His success there won him a fight with Fitzsimmons for the world middleweight championship. This took place on September 26 1894 at the New Orleans Olympic Club for a purse of $5,000. The fight lasted only four minutes before Fitzsimmons whipped three quick lefts into Creedon's handsome nose, despatching the pretender to the canvas and ending the bout.

Left: In a posed publicity shot, Fitzsimmons demonstrates his left-hook on Bob Armstrong.

March 14 1897. Like many before him, 'Gentleman Jim' Corbett thought Fitzsimmons to be over-rated. His confidence seemed well-founded as he was twenty pounds heavier, and the younger man by four years. Corbett did indeed get the better of the early rounds, but gradually began to flag and was caught by a stunning blow to the solar plexus in the fourteenth. Unable to catch his breath and get up, the champion was counted out.

In 1899, Fitzsimmons lost his heavyweight crown at the first defence. James J Jeffries was thirteen years younger and weighed some sixty pounds more than the ageing champion, who broke several bones in his hands attempting to flatten the Californian giant. With incapacitated fists, and completely unable to retaliate against the onslaught, the gallant Fitzsimmons was knocked out in the eleventh round. In a return match three years later, Jeffries confirmed his superiority over Fitzsimmons, who was by this time well past his best, and he overwhelmed the smaller man in eight rounds.

The loss of the heavyweight title did not mean the end for Fitzsimmons, however, and in 1903 he outpointed George Gardner to become world champion of the new light-heavyweight division, thus becoming the first man in history to win three world titles.

Fitzsimmons lost the light-heavyweight title to 'Philadelphia' Jack O'Brien in 1905 but steadfastly refused to give up boxing: he continued to fight until January 29 1914.

Like John J Sullivan before him, Fitzsimmons found acting, or at least appearing in vaudeville shows, a lucrative sideline to boxing. He toured with his own show for a while, but was severely lampooned by critics who wanted to see him fight for real and not in staged acts.

JAMES J CORBETT

James J Corbett's place in boxing history is assured, as he was the first man to win the world heavyweight championship under the Marquess of Queensberry Rules which, amongst other things, demanded that gloves be worn by combatants. He is also remembered because he was one of the first gloved boxers to use his brains as well as his fists; until he introduced a new artistry and skill into boxing, fighters, with rare exceptions such as Mendoza, usually resorted to brawling. Corbett developed his style because he did not possess a particularly telling punch, so he adopted what was in those days an unconventional strategy in which he used his feet to avoid being trapped in the corners. He also stuck out as something of an oddity in the aggressive world of boxing in that he dressed flamboyantly, was quietly spoken, and was unusually well-mannered. He was dubbed 'Gentleman Jim', a not entirely complimentary nickname, by a boxing public that at the time preferred their heroes to be bruising, brawny hulks.

Corbett enjoyed a highly successful amateur boxing career while earning his keep as a San Francisco bank clerk. He turned professional in 1884 with the express intention of ultimately challenging John L Sullivan for the heavyweight title. First, however, he had to prove his mettle by overcoming a local adversary, Joe Choynski. In 1889, Corbett and Choynski had three epic battles under Prize Ring Rules. The first was declared a no contest but the second, which took place on a barge away from the suspicious eyes of the police, resulted in Corbett knocking out Choynski in the twenty-seventh round. After winning the third fight in four rounds, 'Gentleman Jim' challenged the West Indian, Peter Jackson, whom Sullivan had refused to fight because he was black. In 1891, Corbett and Jackson fought

BORN SAN FRANCISCO, CALIFORNIA, SEPTEMBER 1 1866 **TURNED PROFESSIONAL** 1884 **WORLD HEAVYWEIGHT CHAMPION** 1892–1897 **WORLD CHAMPIONSHIP FIGHTS** WON 2, LOST 3 **DIED** LONG ISLAND, FEBRUARY 18 1933

each other for sixty-one rounds, after which both men were exhausted: the fight was declared a no-contest.

The following year Corbett and Sullivan finally met in a New Orleans ring, both wearing five-ounce gloves in accordance with the Queensberry Rules. Sullivan, weighing some forty pounds more than Corbett, was the clear favourite, but the younger man never allowed the 'Boston Strong Boy' to land a heavy punch on him. Instead he gradually wore down the out-of-condition champion by moving around the ring, and in the twenty-first round he unleashed a flurry of blows that knocked Sullivan out.

In 1894, Corbett successfully defended his heavyweight title by knocking out Charlie Mitchell, an Englishman who had unwisely baited the champion, in three rounds. Three years elapsed before he again stepped into a ring and this time his challenger was the ungainly middleweight Bob Fitzsimmons. Corbett under-estimated Fitzsimmons and after winning the early rounds, he began to wane. In the fourteenth round he was floored by a punch to the solar plexus and relinquished his championship title.

Three years after losing the heavyweight crown, which by this time belonged to James J Jeffries, Corbett challenged for it once more. After leading on points, for once in his life he allowed himself to be trapped on the ropes, and Jeffries knocked him out in the twenty-third round. In 1903, he again fought Jeffries for the championship but, at the age of thirty-seven, the task was too much for him and the bout was over in ten rounds.

'Gentleman Jim's' skills were copied and admired by subsequent generations of boxers but the American public never really forgave him for beating their supreme hero, John L Sullivan, and he was never universally popular as a boxer.

Left: Corbett was on the spot in America and ready to challenge for the heavyweight championship while Fitzsimmons was still in Australia. Thus it was Corbett who took the crown from Sullivan. Below: Corbett's great rival Joe Choynski.

Above: Corbett, though not a popular figure, was the darling of the media, and dressed the part. He was the first boxer to acknowledge the role of the heavyweight champion in popular culture by creating an 'image' for himself outside the ring, and he traded on this by building a career on the stage.

Left: The magnificent heavyweight James J Jeffries started in boxing as Corbett's sparring partner, when the latter was in training for his title defence against Fitzsimmons (a fight he was to lose). Ironically, Jeffries, having learnt much from Corbett and turned professional, proved to be Fitzsimmons' first challenger, when, on March 17 1897, the champion eventually decided it was time to defend for the first time a title that he had by then held for over three years. The unfancied Jeffries shocked the boxing world by knocking Fitzsimmons out in the eleventh round, and he proceeded to hold the title until August 1904, when he retired undefeated. His successful defences included a classic bout against Tom Sharkey (by all accounts one of the great fights of all time), a return against Fitzsimmons, and two wins over his old mentor, and now rival, James J Corbett, on May 11 1900 and August 14 1903.

JACK JOHNSON

The title of the most controversial boxer of all time must go to Jack Johnson, the son of a bare-knuckle fighter, who challenged and overcame the supposed superiority of the white man and became the first black heavyweight champion of the world.

Johnson ran away from home when he was twelve and took up work in a racing stables. When he was nineteen, he returned to his home in Galveston and won a fight in a boxing booth at a local fair. This victory was enough to persuade him that it was time to turn professional.

Subsidizing his meagre takings in the ring with occasional work as a painter and decorator, Johnson steadily built up an impressive reputation, and during the next eleven years he disposed of several men who had hopes of the world title. In fact he became so successful that many of the top white fighters ran scared, drawing the so-called 'colour line' and refusing to fight him. Johnson became so incensed that when the reigning world heavyweight champion, the Canadian Tommy Burns, went on a world tour in 1908, he followed in hot pursuit. Burns eventually relented to Johnson's pressure and they fought for the world crown in Sydney, Australia, on Boxing Day 1908.

Johnson relished his opportunity and toyed with the smaller Canadian, taunting him throughout the fight. The police had to declare a halt to the contest in the fourteenth round and Johnson was pronounced the winner, and champion of the world.

Johnson's victory was not well-received in America, and to add fuel to the fire his arrogant behaviour, coupled with the fact that he flirted with white women, made him one of the most unpopular personalities in the country. White America searched for a champion who could dethrone the upstart and Stanley Ketchel, the world middleweight champion, was put forward.

BORN GALVESTON, MARCH 31 1878 **TURNED PROFESSIONAL** 1897 **WORLD HEAVYWEIGHT CHAMPION** 1908–1915 **WORLD CHAMPIONSHIP FIGHTS** WON 6, LOST 1, DREW 1 **DIED** RALEIGH, NORTH CAROLINA, JUNE 10 1946

The 'White Hope' and Johnson are supposed to have come to an agreement that the fight should go the distance so that a lucrative rematch would be assured. The two faced each other in October 1909 in Colma, California, and Ketchel succeeded in putting Johnson on the canvas in the twelfth round. That was enough for Johnson and he smacked Ketchel so hard a few seconds later that, so one version goes, two of the white man's teeth were embedded in Johnson's glove.

The venerable James J Jeffries was brought out of retirement to take on Johnson in 1910, but the referee was obliged to stop the fight in the fifteenth round to prevent the ageing challenger from receiving permanent damage. After one more successful defence against Jim Flynn, in 1912, Johnson fled the United States after he was accused of 'transporting a white woman for immoral purposes' to avoid a one-year prison sentence. He fought two fights in Paris during his exile years and was then persuaded to face Jess Willard. Havana, Cuba, was chosen as the location for the Johnson versus Willard fight as no promoter in the United States dared to stage the contest on home soil. The bout took place on April 5 1915, and the huge cowboy from Kansas knocked out the thirty-seven-year-old Johnson in the twenty-sixth round.

After his defeat, Johnson returned to the United States to serve his prison sentence and he continued to box in exhibitions until he was in his mid-sixties. He died in a car accident at the age of sixty-eight.

Johnson is reckoned by many to be the best heavyweight that ever lived. He developed his defensive skills to a fine degree during the years when he was shunned by the best white boxers, and one of his techniques was to fend off punches with an open left glove before delivering a lethal right upper-cut.

Above: Perennially controversial, Johnson enjoyed nothing more than dressing the part of the gentleman to annoy his racist detractors.

Above: To its shame, the boxing community closed ranks against Johnson, unable to come to terms with the concept of a black champion. Once he had won the championship from Burns, a blatant publicity campaign was launched to find a white man to take it off him. One such, seen here on the canvas, was Stanley Ketchel, who was a victim of Johnson's duplicity, as well as his fists. The story is that the two fighters agreed to go the distance to ensure a lucrative rematch, but that Johnson, having been knocked down by Ketchel, changed his mind and despatched him.

Left: As well as fighting on into his sixties, Johnson also helped fine boxers like Abe Simon.

TOMMY BURNS

A French-Canadian, Tommy Burns is on record as being the shortest man ever to hold the world heavyweight title. He stood just five feet seven inches tall and was never more than a light-heavyweight: yet, with his swift movements and long reach, he beat men far taller and heavier than himself with apparent ease.

When James J Jeffries retired and relinquished his world heavyweight crown in 1905, he arranged a fight between Jack Root and Marvin Hart to decide who should claim the vacant title. Hart won, but his reign was short, as the little-known Burns wrested it from him on February 23 the following year, winning the twenty-round contest on points. However, Burns still did not feel he was getting the recognition he deserved, so he systematically set out to prove his worth. His first defence was in Los Angeles on October 2 1906 against Jim Flynn, whom he knocked out in twelve rounds.

BORN CHESLEY, ONTARIO, JUNE 17 1881
TURNED PROFESSIONAL 1900 **WORLD HEAVYWEIGHT CHAMPION** 1906–1908
WORLD CHAMPIONSHIP FIGHTS WON 12, LOST 1, DREW 1 **DIED** VANCOUVER, MAY 10 1955

This was followed by two battles against 'Philadelphia' Jack O'Brien, also in Los Angeles; the first fight was a twenty-round draw, but Burns won the second on points.

After knocking out Bill Squires in the first round of a bout held during the summer of 1907, Burns travelled to London, England, where he faced the British champion, Gunner Moir, at the National Sporting Club. Moir proved to be no match for the world champion and was knocked out in ten rounds. Staying in London, Burns then had a simple four-round victory over Jack Palmer at the Wonderland arena. To complete a successful tour of Europe, Burns had easy wins over challengers in Dublin and Paris before setting sail for Australia to look for some rich purses.

While he was making this series of comparatively easy defences, Burns was well-aware that there was only one person who could seriously threaten him,

Right: Marvin Hart has the distinction of being the least well-recognized of all the heavyweight champions. His rule started in controversy, when Jeffries decided to retire and, according to some sources (Jeffries himself later denied this), took it on himself to nominate two boxers – Hart and Jack Root – to fight for the succession. Although Hart won the bout, on July 3 1905, and was duly crowned by Jeffries, others thought that better boxers had been ignored. The matter was resolved a few months later when Tommy Burns outpointed Hart in twenty rounds. Burns proceeded to gain outright recognition by defeating all the serious contenders in quick succession.

Left: Burns couldn't keep running for ever: Johnson caught up with him in Sydney, and even though the fight was stopped by the police, Johnson had proved himself so superior that the reluctant authorities had no choice but to award him the fight. Burns had been a worthy champion. His eleven defences were many more than any champion had made to date, and he bowed out with a fortune.

Right: Burns turned to religion and became a preacher. This fascinating letter says: "If I knew what I know today when I was boxing . . . I would never have been a world's champion."

and that was the mighty Jack Johnson. The Canadian was man enough to admit that he stood little chance against the 'Galveston Giant', but he insisted that he wanted to cash in on his title while he still could. The huge American saw it differently, and claimed that Burns was scared to fight. He followed him to Australia, baying for blood.

Realizing that he would have to confront Johnson sooner rather than later, Burns made two quick and conclusive defences of his crown against lesser opponents in the August and September of 1908, and only then agreed to a showdown with Johnson. A huge arena was especially constructed in Sydney for the fight which was scheduled for Boxing Day. When they finally met in the ring, Burns was dwarfed by Johnson, who stood six and a half inches taller and weighed twenty pounds more. He put up a courageous fight but was regarded as a plaything by

Johnson, who taunted him with verbal abuse as well as stinging punches. In the fourteenth round, the police decided to intervene and stop the fight, which was inevitably awarded to Johnson.

Soon after losing to Johnson, Burns gave up boxing for a while to concentrate on managing and promoting, but in 1920 he came out of retirement to challenge the Englishman Joe Beckett, who was British and Commonwealth champion. Aged thirty-nine, his years were against him, and he was stopped by Beckett in seven rounds.

Burns was a shrewd businessman as well as a wily and cunning boxer. He had a hand in promoting many of his own championship fights and he always insisted on seeing his purse money before he got into the ring with an opponent. He invested his considerable fortune wisely and became a wealthy man before being ordained a preacher in 1948.

JIM DRISCOLL

'Peerless' Jim Driscoll ranks as one of the greatest and cleverest boxers never to have been internationally recognized as a world champion. He won every other important title available to him and was only denied the world championship crown because of the ludicrous New York State Frawley Law.

Driscoll was born and brought up in the Welsh city of Cardiff. As a boy he worked in a local newspaper office and legend has it that he used to spar with all-comers protected only by strips of paper wrapped around his hands. He became British featherweight champion in 1907 after knocking out Joe Bowker in the seventeenth round of a contest held at the National Sporting Club, London. It was a title he never lost and he only relinquished it when he retired in 1913. In 1909 he went after Abe Attell, the featherweight world champion, but the wily American insisted that they meet in New York State in a 'no-decision' bout.

At the time boxing in New York was governed by the notorious Frawley Law which permitted boxing, but only on the condition that no decision was made at the end of the fight. This meant that all matches were effectively exhibition bouts and the only way a man could win was to knock out an opponent. Members of the press in attendance could give their verdicts on a fight but their decisions held no sway with the ruling bodies. Champions took advantage of this law and readily defended their titles in New York, safe in the knowledge that all they had to do to retain their crowns was to stay upright through the scheduled number of rounds.

Driscoll had just about everything a boxer requires, but he was not renowned for his punching power. Throughout their ten-round fight, he comprehensively out-boxed Attell, who frequently missed his target altogether. However Attell survived, and

BORN CARDIFF, DECEMBER 15 1881 **TURNED PROFESSIONAL** 1899 **DIED** CARDIFF, JANUARY 31 1925

therefore retained his title. The press gave a unanimous verdict in Driscoll's favour but it was not enough to make him champion. But back in Britain, and particularly in Wales, he was regarded as the uncrowned champion of the world.

Returning home across the Atlantic, Driscoll won the first featherweight Lonsdale Belt match on stopping Seaman Hayes in six rounds. He went on to make the treasured belt his own property by humbling Spike Robson in two subsequent contests. Driscoll's darkest day came in December 1910 when he was pitted against fellow Welshman Freddy Welsh in Cardiff. The fight for the British lightweight title turned dirty and Driscoll lost his temper, butting Welsh in the tenth round and earning a disqualification.

In June 1912 Driscoll knocked out the Frenchman, Jean Poesy, in twelve rounds at the National Sporting Club, and became European featherweight champion. He successfully defended his new title in a twenty-round draw against Owen Moran and retired from the ring in 1913.

During World War One he became an army physical education instructor, but, short of cash, decided to make a comeback when the war ended. He had two wins before meeting the Frenchman, Charles Ledoux, at his favourite venue, the National Sporting Club. Driscoll had the best of the early rounds but in the sixteenth was caught by a flurry of blows from the hard-hitting Frenchman and was forced to retire.

Driscoll earned the nickname 'Peerless' because of his mastery in the ring. He was technically superb, particularly in defence, and Ledoux, who was eleven years his junior, had the grace to pay him a tribute after his victory. Driscoll was, in fact, already a sick man when he fought Ledoux, and he died of consumption five years later.

Above: Freddie Welsh (1886–1927) was a great rival of Driscoll's, and their 1910 fight is one of the dirtiest on record, causing bitterness and resentment for years afterwards. Welsh won the world crown from Willie Ritchie in 1914 – an achievement Driscoll could never match.

Left: Driscoll, called 'Peerless' because of his artistry and neatness, is one of Britain's greatest unsung sporting heroes. He was undisputed British featherweight champion for six years, and no challenger could get close to him, but he was consistently frustrated in his attempts to get world championship contests with American fighters. When he did, he wiped the floor with Abe Attell (by common agreement), but a State law turned his mastery of the champion into an insignificant exhibition bout.

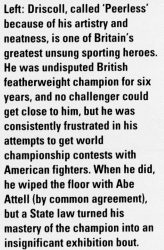

Above: Abe Attell was, like Driscoll, a fighter more renowned for skill than power – which didn't prevent him from scoring more than forty-five knock-out victories in his career. Born in 1884, he held the world featherweight crown between April 30 1908 and February 22 1912.

Left: Forced out of retirement by financial problems, Driscoll (on the right) puts up a brave but hopeless struggle against Ledoux in his last fight.

SAM LANGFORD

One of the most talented boxers never to win a world championship was Sam Langford who, during his peak years, was denied opportunities to challenge for the ultimate crown because of the colour of his skin. Langford was born and brought up in Canada but moved south to the United States to seek his fortune and there turned professional in 1902.

Langford began his professional career as a featherweight and had a notable success in his second year when he beat Joe Gans who had at one time held the world lightweight title. Although he was small, standing no more than five feet seven and a half inches, and comparatively light, Langford was ambitious and craved the heavyweight title above all else. To his chagrin, however, he was consistently refused fights with the leading white heavyweight

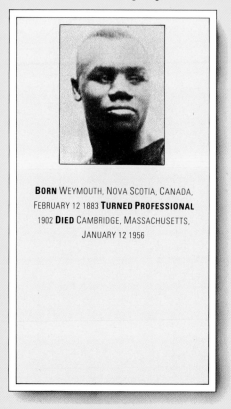

BORN WEYMOUTH, NOVA SCOTIA, CANADA, FEBRUARY 12 1883 **TURNED PROFESSIONAL** 1902 **DIED** CAMBRIDGE, MASSACHUSETTS, JANUARY 12 1956

contenders. As a consequence he was forced to fight his fellow blacks and was obliged to take on the same people over and over again. He had an extraordinary catalogue of twenty-three battles against Harry Wills, fifteen against Sam McVey, fourteen against Joe Jeanette and eleven tough encounters against Jeff Clarke.

In 1906, he was pitched against the 'Galveston Giant', Jack Johnson, and gave the man who was to become the first ever black world heavyweight champion the fight of his life. Johnson won on a narrow points decision; he was so surprised at Langford's talent that he was afraid to box him again and steadfastly refused offers of a return contest, however hard Langford and his managers pushed.

Johnson became world champion in 1908 but proved to be so unpopular with the white American public that, if anything, he made it

Above: Langford knocks Bill Lang clear through the ropes.

Left: 'Iron' Bill Hague, the British champion, was no push-over, but Langford gave him a boxing lesson in 1909 before disposing of him in the fourth round.

more difficult than ever for black heavyweights to rise to the top. Nevertheless, the 'Boston Tar Baby', as Langford was dubbed, was at last allowed to fight white men, and he disposed of such 'white hopes' as Jim Barry, Jim Flynn, Sandy Ferguson and Tony Ross. In 1909, Langford crossed the Atlantic and took on the British champion, 'Iron' Hague. He put on an impressive display of skill and knocked the Englishman out in the fourth round.

To boost his career still further, Langford moved to Australia, where he lived for more than a year,

Right: Langford got to know Harry Wills pretty well during his career: they fought one another no less than twenty-three times. They had to fight each other because the leading white contenders and champions were persistently allowed to refuse fights with black boxers with the tacit approval of the authorities. Fighters such as Langford, Wills, McVey, and Jeanette were undoubtedly superior to most of the so-called 'Great White Hopes', but the prejudices of the times denied them the fame and riches of the world stage.

fighting ten contests and winning all but one of them. However with his years working against him, and with the world crown in the grasp of the reluctant Johnson, his hope of a title bout diminished.

The record books show that Langford only ever held one heavyweight title, the Mexican. He won that crown when he flattened Jim Savage in the opening round of a bout held in Mexico City in 1923. By that time, though, he was past forty and his best boxing years were behind him. He refused to retire, however, and continued to fight until he was forty-four. He would have continued further had his eyesight not been blighted by cataracts which rendered him partially blind.

Tragically, Langford's eyes continued to fail him and not long after his last fight he was completely unable to see. Thankfully, his many friends rallied round and saved him from a life of poverty, and before he died in early 1956 he at least had the satisfaction of knowing that he had been elected to *The Ring*'s Hall of Fame.

In his professional career Langford fought close to 400 contests, and, although he only weighed 145 pounds, most of his fights were against heavyweights. He owed his success to his massive shoulders and extraordinarily long reach.

GEORGES CARPENTIER

Georges Carpentier, dubbed the 'Pride of Paris', was the darling of France during his heyday and was fêted like a movie star by his adoring public. Yet, for all his debonair charm, he had humble beginnings, being the son of a miner. He started to box as a flyweight in his early teens and during his career he gradually progressed right up to heavyweight.

Carpentier won the French national lightweight title when he was just fifteen and he was still short of his eighteenth birthday when he clinched the European welterweight title. In 1913, he stepped up to heavyweight and got the better of the British champion, Bombardier Billy Wells, in a contest that lasted four rounds. After a repeat victory against Wells, he fought the American, Ed 'Gunboat' Smith, in London, for the 'white' heavyweight world championship (the genuine champion, Jack Johnson, was black, and at that time there was a scandalous attempt in the boxing world to seek a white boxer to beat him). Smith was disqualified in the sixth round but, as the contest was fought just before the outbreak of World War One, Carpentier was unable to capitalize on his victory. Instead, he joined the French Air Force and had a distinguished career during the war, winning the *Croix de Guerre* and the *Médaille Militaire*.

The war deprived Carpentier of his peak years but nevertheless, in 1920, he travelled to Jersey City to take on 'Battling' Levinsky for the world light-heavyweight championship. He got the better of the American in four rounds and the manner in which he fought convinced the promoter, Tex Rickard, that he was a worthy opponent for the world heavyweight champion, Jack Dempsey.

Conceding twenty-four pounds in weight, Carpentier faced Dempsey in a huge, purpose-built

BORN LENS, FRANCE, JANUARY 12 1894 **TURNED PROFESSIONAL** 1908 **WORLD LIGHT-HEAVYWEIGHT CHAMPION** 1920– 1922 **WORLD CHAMPIONSHIP FIGHTS** (MIDDLEWEIGHT) LOST 1 (LIGHT-HEAVYWEIGHT) WON 2, LOST 1 (HEAVY-WEIGHT) LOST 1 **DIED** PARIS, OCTOBER 28 1975

arena on Boyle's Thirty Acres, New Jersey, in 1921. More than 80,000 fans turned out to view the fight which became the first in history to gross more than $1 million at the gate. During the contest the brave Frenchman broke his thumb, which dramatically affected his punching power, and he was pulverized into defeat in the fourth round.

In May the following year Carpentier defended his light-heavyweight world title against Ted 'Kid' Lewis in London. He won in the first round but in controversial circumstances, the Englishman claiming that he was knocked out by an illegal blow. Four months after defeating Lewis, Carpentier fought the unknown Senegalese fighter, 'Battling' Siki in Paris. Carpentier and his manager, François Descamps, thought the fight would be an easy one but they were sorely mistaken. Carpentier had the better of the opening rounds but Siki, who was short of talent but extremely brave, badly damaged the handsome Frenchman's nose in the fourth round. Thereafter the challenger pummelled Carpentier and during the sixth round, Descamps threw in the towel. Whether out of loyalty to the champion or not, the referee ignored the towel and disqualified Siki for allegedly tripping Carpentier. The crowd was outraged and, amid booing, the decision was reversed in Siki's favour.

Carpentier was never the same after losing his world title to Siki. He beat the British heavyweight champion, Joe Beckett, for a second time in 1923, but during a tour of the United States in 1924 lost to Gene Tunney in the fifteenth round. In 1927 he quit boxing and retired to run a café in Paris.

Carpentier was a master of the ring, being a quick mover with a devastating right-hand punch that accounted for many of his opponents. He was a suave and charming man, and a hero in his beloved France.

Left: The charming Frenchman with his equally dapper manager, François Descamps, arriving in New York to prepare for Dempsey.

Top: The scene at the Thirty Acres Oval seconds before the Carpentier v Dempsey title fight commenced. The two boxers have returned to their corners after the preliminaries; the referee is Harry Ertle. Above: Carpentier damaged a thumb early in the fight, and this, combined with the amount of weight he was giving away, saw him going backwards virtually from the start. Here in the fourth, Dempsey has Carpentier reeling over the ropes. Right: Later in the fourth, and it is all over. Carpentier stayed down.

Above: The Carpentier/Dempsey fight was the first million-dollar battle in boxing history. Tex Rickard promoted the fight, and constructed a special arena on Boyle's Thirty Acres to hold the crowds his publicity drew.

TED 'KID' LEWIS

Gershon Mendeloff, who changed his name to Ted Lewis and was known as 'Kid', was born of Jewish parents in the heart of London's East End. He turned professional when he was just fourteen years old and went on to become one of the most successful and admired boxers ever to have been produced by England.

Lewis started as a featherweight, and in 1913 won the British title in a contest held at the illustrious National Sporting Club. A year later he went one better and picked up the European title, but was forced to give up both championships after he put on too much weight. Late in 1914 he travelled to Australia where he fought five twenty-round contests in nine weeks: then, fighting as a welterweight, he moved on to try his luck and skill in the United States.

Lewis became the undisputed world welterweight champion on beating the New Yorker, Jack Britton,

BORN LONDON, OCTOBER 24 1894 **TURNED PROFESSIONAL** 1909 **WORLD WELTERWEIGHT CHAMPION** 1915–1916, 1917–1919 **WORLD CHAMPIONSHIP FIGHTS** (WELTERWEIGHT) WON 5, LOST 3, NO-DECISION 2 (LIGHT-HEAVYWEIGHT) LOST 1 **DIED** LONDON, OCTOBER 20 1970

in August 1915. He again got the better of Britton the following month, but in a third clash, in 1916, he lost the decision in a twenty-round contest. The Londoner regained the title from his long-time adversary in 1917 and held on to it for two years. He successfully defended the championship four times, with two victories and two no-decision bouts, before being knocked out by Britton in nine rounds on March 17 1919. After this defeat Lewis returned to his roots in London.

Back on home territory Lewis was unbeatable. He knocked out Johnny Basham to win the British Empire and European welterweight titles in June 1920, and, full of confidence, he crossed the Atlantic once more in an attempt to wrest the welterweight world crown from none other than Jack Britton. Britton again proved to be too strong for the Englishman and won on points in front of his home crowd in New York.

Right: Lewis shakes hands with Jack Britton, but the civilities between these two great rivals were never more than cursory. Lewis was, to many critics, the finest British boxer of the twentieth century, and remains the only fighter from Britain to have won the genuine respect and approval of American fight fans and commentators. This reputation was founded on his twenty contests with the only welterweight of the time who could compare with him – Jack Britton. During Lewis' five-year stay in the States the title changed hands regularly between them: they once fought three times in less than three weeks.

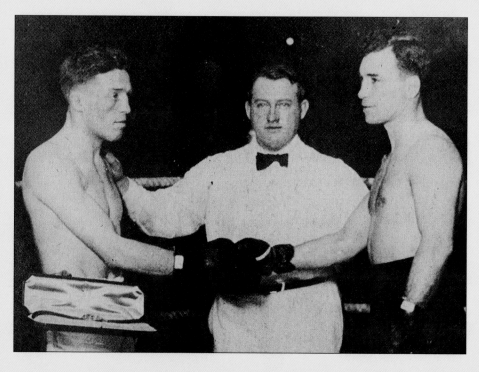

This was the last time these two great boxers met in the ring. In all they fought each other twenty times, including six championships bouts: these had the honours split, with both men winning three contests.

Returning once again to Europe, Lewis subdued Jack Bloomfield to win the British and European middleweight crowns, and in June 1922 he relieved the Australian, Frankie Burns, of the Empire middleweight title. In May 1922 Lewis fought the Frenchman, Georges Carpentier, for the world light-heavyweight championship in London and lost in controversial circumstances in the opening round. By his own account, Lewis was angered by Carpentier's holding, and turned to the referee to complain. While doing this, he dropped his guard and Carpentier landed a right-hand smack on his chin.

Lewis continued to fight after his brief encounter with Carpentier but he was never the force he had been. Roland Todd took the British and Empire middleweight titles from him in 1923 and Tommy Milligan beat him on points in 1924 to clinch his British and Empire welterweight crowns.

Lewis finally retired at the age of thirty-five and briefly flirted with a show-business career in a vaudeville act. He later became a boxing coach and an ever-popular figure in British boxing circles. Lewis won innumerable fans both in England and in the United States for his courageous, all-action style. He was rarely forced into retreat and his preferred tactic was to press forward with both fists flailing.

Above: Australia's Frankie Burns does his best to avoid a swinging right from a Lewis in typically aggressive form. Lewis knocked out Burns in the eleventh round at Holland Park in London on June 19 1922 to win the Empire middleweight championship.
Right: The 'Kid' in his prime.

JACK DEMPSEY

Born into an impoverished family, William Harrison Dempsey followed an elder brother's footsteps when he took up boxing. He adopted the name Jack after the famous 'Nonpareil' Jack Dempsey, the middleweight champion from the end of the nineteenth century. The new Jack Dempsey was born in the same year that the great old-timer passed away.

He honed his skills to perfection while working in local mining and lumber camps where life was tough and fights were frequent. His big break came when he was spotted by Jack 'Doc' Kearns, who became his manager, confidant and publicist. Under the guidance of Kearns he fought a series of carefully chosen fights that brought him into contention for the world championship.

Dempsey faced the champion, Jess Willard, on July 4 1919 and Kearns was so confident of his man that he bet Dempsey's entire purse of $27,500, at odds of ten to one, that he would win in one round. Dempsey very nearly became a rich man overnight. He knocked Willard down seven times in the opening round and was jumping out of the ring to collect his winnings when he was summoned back: the bell had sounded but in all the commotion nobody had heard it. Dempsey lost his purse but had the consolation of becoming world champion in the third round when the humiliated Willard retired.

Nicknamed the 'Manassa Mauler', the new champion knocked out Billy Miske and Bill Brennan the following year and then in 1921 the entrepreneur Tex Rickard promoted the first 'fight of the century', pitting Dempsey against the Frenchman, Georges Carpentier, who was the European champion. Rickard built a special arena for the contest at Jersey City and some 80,000 people flocked to see the contest, paying well over $1 million at the gate. The gallant Carpentier

BORN MANASSA, COLORADO, JUNE 24 1895
TURNED PROFESSIONAL 1914 WORLD
HEAVYWEIGHT CHAMPION 1919–1926
WORLD CHAMPIONSHIP FIGHTS WON 6,
LOST 2 DIED NEW YORK, MAY 31 1983

broke his thumb during the ferocious struggle in the ring and was knocked out in the fourth round.

Dempsey's next fight was not until 1923 when he easily outpointed Tommy Gibbons over fifteen rounds. Searching for suitable opposition for the champion, Rickard then produced the Argentinian, Luis Firpo, a giant of a man who had a formidable punch. Dempsey knocked Firpo to the canvas no less than seven times in the opening round but the courageous Argentinian retaliated by knocking the 'Manassa Mauler' through the ropes and into the ranks of pressmen. In the second round Firpo could not find any strength and was finished off by the champion.

The phenomenally successful Kearns–Dempsey partnership ended acrimoniously after the Firpo fight, the manager disapproving of the champion's marriage to the actress Estelle Taylor. Dempsey did not fight for three years and when he did he was in for a surprise. Gene Tunney took advantage of the champion's long spell away from the ring and convincingly beat him on points over ten rounds at Philadelphia in September 1926. The rematch almost exactly a year later ended in the same result but not before Dempsey had felled Tunney in the seventh round. This was the famous 'Long Count' when the referee did not start counting until Dempsey had retreated to a neutral corner. Tunney was in fact down for fourteen seconds, the extra four giving him enough time to recover and win the fight.

After his second fight with Tunney Dempsey retired to become a successful businessman. He will always be remembered for being a fighter in every sense of the word who had a clubbing punch in both fists. He was one of the greatest box-office draws of all time and five of his fights attracted more than $1 million at the gate – an extraordinary amount at the time.

Above: Looking here like a cross between a choirboy and an ad-man's dream, it is hard to believe that to most fight-fans Dempsey is emblematic of the twenties tough guy: the kid from the backstreets who made it to fame and fortune through a mixture of need and brute power. His life reads like a script for the archetypal boxing movie: flushed with his sudden status he is seduced away to Hollywood, where his new film-star wife edges out mentor 'Doc' Kearns; returning to the ring, he finds he does not have it any more, and lets clean-cut Gene Tunney walk off with his crown.

Top: Dempsey pulls another million-dollar crowd for the return against ex-Marine Tunney.

Above: One of Dempsey's finest hours. Matched as a relative unknown against champion Jess Willard, he put together a twenty-punch combination in the third that pummelled the older man to defeat. When he opened his Broadway restaurant, he had a whole wall painted with a mural of this scene.

Left: Dempsey persuades another great old-timer, Jack Sharkey, to play Willard's role in front of the famous painting.

GENE TUNNEY

Like many great champions, Gene Tunney came from a relatively poor family: he was born in Greenwich Village on Manhattan Island, New York. As a teenager he proved that he was highly intelligent and his parents had hopes of him taking up a literary career. However, the young Tunney dashed their aspirations and elected to become a professional boxer when he was eighteen.

Tunney sailed through his first fourteen fights undefeated but was then drafted into the United States Marine Corps. Far from wrecking his boxing hopes, the army positively boosted them, and he made a name for himself by winning the United States Expeditionary Force's light-heavyweight championship while stationed in France in 1919. It was at this time that Tunney first realised that he had the talent and power to be champion.

On returning to the United States after his army service, Tunney went back to his chosen profession full-time, and won twenty-two consecutive fights inside two years. At the beginning of 1922 he relieved the veteran 'Battling' Levinsky of the American light-heavyweight title but four months later lost it to Harry Greb. This was Tunney's only defeat in his professional career and it had a massive influence on his approach to boxing. He was obliged to spend a week in bed after the savage beating Greb gave him, but, instead of giving up, he spent the time hatching a tactical plan to beat his assailant. His plot worked to perfection and he got the better of Greb, the 'Pittsburgh Windmill', on four subsequent meetings.

With renewed confidence, Tunney began to take on heavyweights and achieved astonishing success. In 1924 he beat the great Frenchman, Georges Carpentier, in the fifteenth round of a bout at Yankee Stadium, and he gradually eliminated all the contenders for the world heavyweight crown. By 1926 Jack Dempsey had been world heavyweight champion for seven years: he agreed to a challenge from Tunney, and the two confronted each other in Philadelphia on September 23. Boxing cleverly, Tunney achieved his boyhood ambition and convincingly outpointed the 'Manassa Mauler', whom many had thought was unbeatable.

Tunney gave Dempsey a return match in Chicago the following year, and very nearly lost his title in the seventh round when Dempsey floored him. However, in one of the most notorious incidents in all of boxing history, Dempsey made the critical error of not immediately retreating to a neutral corner, and crucial seconds ticked away before the referee started the count. Tunney was in fact down for fourteen seconds and he recovered to win the ten-round fight on points. Talking about the 'Long Count' issue later, Tunney maintained that he could have got up in ten seconds and that it was his privilege to make the most of the count. In all truth, Dempsey only had himself to blame – he knew the rules well enough.

Tunney made only one more defence of his title before retiring. That was against the New Zealander, Tom Heeney, at Yankee Stadium in 1928. Heeney was stopped in eleven rounds and the fight proved to be something of a damp squib and never captured the imagination of the American public.

Tunney was one of the shrewdest of heavyweight boxers and he studied his opponents meticulously before he met them. On retiring, the undefeated champion was a wealthy man, having won nearly $1 million in his second fight with Dempsey alone. He married the heiress Polly Lauder and became a highly successful businessman, listing among his friends such figures as George Bernard Shaw.

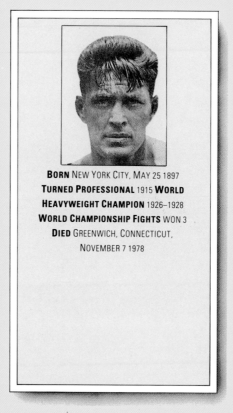

BORN NEW YORK CITY, MAY 25 1897
TURNED PROFESSIONAL 1915 **WORLD HEAVYWEIGHT CHAMPION** 1926–1928
WORLD CHAMPIONSHIP FIGHTS WON 3
DIED GREENWICH, CONNECTICUT, NOVEMBER 7 1978

Above: Still remembered by some fans as the greatest fight ever, the return between Tunney and Dempsey on September 22 1927 at Soldiers' Field, Chicago, had it all. With an eye for publicity, the promoter set the fight exactly a year and a day after Tunney's skill had won the title from Dempsey's aggression: so great was the excitement that the crowds filled the box-office coffers to a level that would not be matched for decades – $2,658,000 was taken, of which Tex Rickard personally pocketed over half a million. But above all, the fight was controversial: it was 'The Battle of the Long Count'. In the seventh, Dempsey floored Tunney, but failed to retire to a neutral corner to the satisfaction of referee Dave Barry. In the confusion, Tunney was down for, according to most sources, between fourteen and sixteen seconds. It is history that he recovered and went on to win a points result.

Left: Tunney at his peak. Unlike most champions, he coped well with the wealth and fame: he was a cultured man who mixed with writers and artists; he succeeded in business, and he saw one of his sons enter Congress.

Above: Dempsey and Tunney were still receiving recognition for their epic battles over thirty years later.

MICKEY WALKER

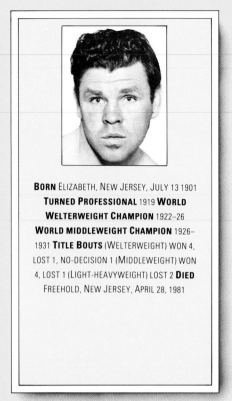

BORN ELIZABETH, NEW JERSEY, JULY 13 1901 **TURNED PROFESSIONAL** 1919 **WORLD WELTERWEIGHT CHAMPION** 1922–26 **WORLD MIDDLEWEIGHT CHAMPION** 1926–1931 **TITLE BOUTS** (WELTERWEIGHT) WON 4, LOST 1, NO-DECISION 1 (MIDDLEWEIGHT) WON 4, LOST 1 (LIGHT-HEAVYWEIGHT) LOST 2 **DIED** FREEHOLD, NEW JERSEY, APRIL 28, 1981

Known as the 'Toy Bulldog', as much for his tenacious fighting skills as for his facial features, Mickey Walker was Irish-American born, and was brought up in a tough district of New Jersey. He turned professional at the earliest opportunity and fought some forty-five bouts before earning the right to challenge the ageing Jack Britton for the world welterweight title. He eventually beat Britton on a points decision on November 1 1922 in New York.

Walker had successfully defended his welterweight title three times (one no-decision against Pete Latzo) when he took on Harry Greb for the middleweight crown in 1925. Greb won the New York fight on points and legend has it that Walker pursued Greb after the contest and the two of them continued to brawl in Times Square (this scrap lasted only a few seconds).

After one more successful defence of his welterweight title against Dave Shade, the 'Toy Bulldog' lost it to Pete Latzo in May 1926. The press had a field day on that occasion, as a rumour spread around that

Walker had entered the ring nursing a severe hangover. Headache or not, he managed to stay on his feet for ten rounds before losing on points.

Walker almost retired after being knocked out by Joe Dundee in a fight that followed the Latzo contest, but he was persuaded to keep going. He was not too upset at relinquishing his welterweight title as he had a tendency to put on weight and he set his sights on gaining the middleweight world championship. He achieved his ambition by outpointing 'Tiger' Flowers in Chicago on December 3 1926. He went on to defend his new title three times but, deciding to chase bigger fish, he gave it up in 1931 to concentrate fully on the heavier divisions.

Walker had two attempts at winning the light-heavyweight championship of the world, but lost on points on both occasions: first against Tommy Loughran in 1929, and then against Maxie Rosenbloom in 1933. Ironically, he outpointed Rosenbloom the following year in a non-title contest.

Forever ambitious, Walker still openly coveted the

Right: 'Tiger' Flowers took the middleweight title off Harry Greb on February 26 1926, and defended it in a return match on August 26 of the same year. He was the first black boxer to hold the crown at this weight. Flowers met Walker in Chicago on December 3 1926, and was relieved of the championship on a points decision after ten hard rounds. Walker remained champion until 1931.

Left: Not content with his great successes as a middleweight, Walker's ambitions constantly led him to challenge the giants of the ring, such as Jack Sharkey. His dream was the heavyweight championship: predictably, he never got close – he was giving away much too much in height, reach, and weight. His finest achievement outside the middleweight bracket was his draw against Sharkey, a rugged boxer who on June 21 1932 was to gain a points result over Max Schmeling to gain the heavyweight championship.

heavyweight title above all else. This was particularly foolhardy as he stood no more than five feet seven inches tall and weighed little more than one hundred and sixty-eight pounds at his heaviest. Still, he had some success against the big men and managed to hold the future world heavyweight champion, Jack Sharkey, to a draw. Against the rising Max Schmeling, however, he met his match and was pummelled into an eight-round defeat.

Walker was hugely popular with the American public and media during his heyday. Not only was he a ferocious and fearless fighter who was prepared to take on anybody, but he was also a flamboyant character who provided the press with a succession of juicy stories. He was an inveterate womanizer and he often liked to drink until dawn. He married seven times, including three remarriages, and his extravagant lifestyle was a considerable burden on his finances. However his manager was the wily Jack 'Doc' Kearns who amassed him a considerable fortune over their years together.

When he retired in 1935, the 'Toy Bulldog' took up the more passive art of painting, adopting a 'primitive' style. His canvases were widely acclaimed and he had several important exhibitions. More predictably, he also owned a popular bar sited, fittingly enough, next to Madison Square Garden in New York, the scene of many of his greatest triumphs.

Above: Walker challenged Tommy Loughran for the world light-heavyweight championship, but was out-gunned. Walker's obsession with boxing above his weight inevitably took its toll: it drained him of strength, and prevented him from fulfilling his full potential against boxers in his own class. At the same time it made him a hero with the public: they loved him for his courage and his attitude. **Left:** Mickey Walker, the boxer's boxer. He would fight anyone, anytime, and refused to believe that size counted for anything inside the ring.

MAX SCHMELING

Max Schmeling had a long and controversial professional career that spanned more than twenty years. He started out as a light-heavyweight and gained international recognition when he knocked out the Belgian, Fernand Delarge, in June 1927. This fourteen-round victory made him European champion and he successfully defended the title against Hein Domgoerger on November 6 1927.

In 1928 Schmeling moved up to heavyweight and began a campaign in the United States which had an impressive start, with five consecutive victories. The world title had by this time been vacated by the retiring Gene Tunney and in 1930 the two leading contenders, Schmeling and Jack Sharkey, were matched against each other to decide who should have the title. The fight took place in Yankee Stadium, and during the fourth round, Schmeling was dumped on to the canvas. While the German was being carried to his corner, his manager, Joe Jacobs, protested to the referee that the telling punch had been a foul, and a ringside judge agreed that it had landed below the belt. As a result Schmeling was declared the champion and went into the history books as the first heavyweight to win the ultimate crown on a foul.

In July 1931 Schmeling saw off the challenge of Young Stribling when the referee was obliged to call a halt in the fifteenth round. The following year, Sharkey was granted a return match with Schmeling and this time the contest went the full fifteen rounds. However, the outcome, a points victory to the American, did not seem entirely fair, even to the partisan American audience, and prompted Joe Jacobs to sob, 'We was robbed.'

Schmeling's first bout after losing his heavyweight title was against the gallant Mickey Walker, former welter- and middleweight world champion. In the

BORN BRANDENBURG, GERMANY, SEPTEMBER 28 1905 **TURNED PROFESSIONAL** 1924 **WORLD HEAVYWEIGHT CHAMPION** 1930–1932 **WORLD CHAMPIONSHIP FIGHTS** WON 2, LOST 2

eighth round of an all-action tussle in which fortunes fluctuated both ways, Schmeling felled the American and begged the referee to halt the fight. After several more knockdowns he was declared the winner.

The two fights for which Schmeling will always be remembered were against Joe Louis. The first took place in New York on June 19 1936. Louis was the over-riding favourite to win the non-title fight, but Schmeling was nothing if not clever, and he outwitted the 'Brown Bomber', ultimately sending him to the canvas in the twelfth round. The return contest two years later was rather different. Louis was by this time world champion and tensions ran high: the Nazi propaganda machine was at its peak, and the contest was seen as a battle between the black and white races as much as for the world crown. The fight was over within one round, Schmeling being decked by a devastatingly ferocious onslaught from the American.

Returning to Germany after his fight against Louis, Schmeling won the European heavyweight title against his fellow countryman, Adolf Heuser, in 1939. Soon after this one-round victory World War Two started, and Schmeling became a paratrooper in the German army. When hostilities ceased in 1945 he made a brief comeback but after a couple of wins he was beaten by Walter Neusel in 1948 and decided that it was time to retire from the ring.

It has been alleged that Schmeling had leanings towards the Nazi Party. It is certainly true that he met Hitler and he was once photographed giving the infamous Nazi salute before a fight in Germany. However, he always maintained, and most agree, that he was neither a racist nor a Nazi. When he quit boxing, he started several successful ventures and maintained close links with contacts in the United States, where he remained a respected and popular figure.

Left: Schmeling had held the heavyweight crown for a brief period six years earlier, having beaten Jack Sharkey to take up the vacant title. But this, undoubtedly, was his finest hour. Joe Louis was still new on the scene, but was commonly regarded as a future champion who would be one of the all time greats. Schmeling was matched against him as a mature opponent who would provide experience, but no threat. Unfortunately, they forgot to give Schmeling the script, and he proceeded to take the youngster apart, felling him finally in the twelfth.

Right: The eighth round of a famous fight: Schmeling v Walker on September 26 1932. Still recalled by fans as one of the greatest slugging matches of all time, it was a typical instance of Walker never knowing when he was beaten. By the eighth, Schmeling's huge weight advantage had taken full toll, and, as Walker went down, he begged referee Denny to end the bout, which he eventually did.

Above: Two years after their first fight, Louis was champion, and not about to repeat his earlier error. Nobody imagined that so much damage could be done by one man to another in just over two minutes. Schmeling went down three times, and didn't get up on the third.

MAX BAER

BORN OMAHA, NEBRASKA, FEBRUARY 11 1909
TURNED PROFESSIONAL 1929 **WORLD HEAVYWEIGHT CHAMPION** 1934–1935
WORLD CHAMPIONSHIP FIGHTS WON 1, .OST 1 **DIED** HOLLYWOOD, NOVEMBER 21 1959

Max Baer possessed one of the most devastating right hands that boxing has ever known, but he never truly capitalized on it, and his fickle temperament often let him down. He was the son of a tough Californian cattle butcher and legend has it that he only discovered his punching power when a man made an inappropriate comment as he walked his girl-friend home one evening. Baer was so incensed at the remark, and the insult to his girl, that he knocked the hapless individual clean through a shop door.

Turning professional at twenty, Baer had the hallmarks of a potential champion. He was a fearsome puncher, and he also had an impressive physique, though he lacked natural boxing skills. After a succession of impressive knockout wins he rose sufficiently high up the ladder to earn a fight with the former world champion, Max Schmeling.

The contest, held at Yankee Stadium in 1933, was close until Baer unleashed his right hand and stopped the German in the tenth round. This victory earned Baer a title bout against the Italian Primo Carnera. The Carnera versus Baer contest took place on June 14 1934 and turned into an almost comic spectacle. Carnera was an enormous man who lacked a heavy punch but was not short on skill. He weighed fifty pounds more than Baer, who found it easy to manoeuvre his way around the ponderous giant, landing blows at will. In all, the American floored the Italian eleven times in eleven rounds before the Italian decided he had taken enough punishment, and called a halt to the proceedings.

Baer's tragedy was that he could take nothing seriously and he even joked and played the comic during his fight against Carnera. He rarely bothered

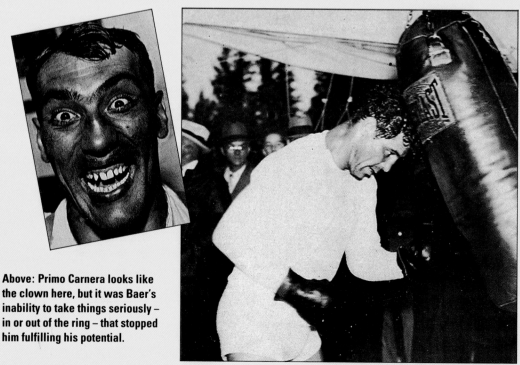

Above: Primo Carnera looks like the clown here, but it was Baer's inability to take things seriously – in or out of the ring – that stopped him fulfilling his potential.

Left: A rare picture of Baer training. Baer was finally shocked into realising that boxing was a serious business when he lost the title on his first defence to the unrated Braddock – a fighter who was over-the-hill and who had been given no chance against Baer's firepower. For once in his life he went into training, aiming to pick off Joe Louis and start a comeback trail. Unfortunately Louis' talent was just coming into its prime: even an in-shape Baer stood no chance, and he went down in four.

to train and relied solely on his right-hand punch to win fights. His come-uppance came a year later when, on June 13 1935, he faced James J Braddock on Long Island, New York. Braddock, who had lost a light-heavyweight title contest against Tommy Loughran in 1929, was given virtually no chance against Baer's punch but he used his brain and steered clear of trouble, eventually outpointing the champion in one of the biggest upsets in heavyweight boxing history.

Shocked by his defeat at the hands of the ageing Braddock, Baer attempted to fight his way back to the top but this time he did not find it so easy to compete against some of the best heavyweights of the time. Joe Louis knocked him out in four rounds, a defeat that he found hard to stomach, and England's Tommy Farr outpointed him in London in 1937. In a return fight in New York a year later, Baer got the better of Farr but more trouble loomed for the former champion in the shape of Lou Nova. Baer fought Nova twice, once in 1939 and again in 1941. On both occasions he was stopped inside the distance and after the second fight he finally decided to retire.

Baer was one of the most popular of all American boxers for two reasons. Firstly, he thrilled audiences during his heyday by regularly knocking opponents flat on the canvas and, secondly, he was a natural clown who revelled in playing the fool. He had the talent and ability to become a truly great champion but discovered that being a high-profile playboy was more to his liking. He became a radio personality and made a film called *The Prize Fighter and the Lady* (1933), in which he starred with Jack Dempsey.

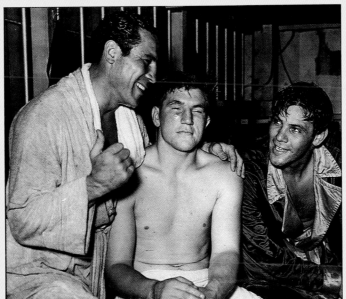

Right: Baer's defeat by Louis placed him firmly in the second division: as Louis was a one-man first division at the time, it was a situation he shared with virtually every other would-be contender. He is seen here with Tommy Farr (centre) the English champion with whom he fought two terrific battles, and with his brother Buddy (far right). Both Farr and Buddy Baer gave Louis tough fights (Buddy actually flooring the champ in the first of their two meetings), but the 'Brown Bomber' was unbeatable when they were at their best.

Above: If a film had been made about Baer's life in the thirties, the leading role would have been played by Errol Flynn. Baer had it all: speed, timing, strength, and a great punch for use inside the ring; and looks, physique and wit to apply outside it. All he lacked was dedication. The crowds adored him – any Baer fight, even after his defeats by Braddock and Louis, was an event and a spectacle. But in the end, he enjoyed life too much to make the sacrifices necessary to become a great fighter rather than a great personality.

HENRY ARMSTRONG

The eleventh child of a family of fifteen children, Henry Armstrong could boast that a potent mixture of Negro, Cherokee Indian and Irish blood flowed through his veins. He was born Henry Jackson and was brought up in a poor quarter of St Louis where, as a teenager, he boxed for trophies which he invariably sold to help keep his large family in food. At nineteen he left home and journeyed to Los Angeles, where he intended to make his fortune. Initially he earned his keep in California by boxing to orders: he got paid for winning, drawing or, most frequently, for deliberately losing fights that were promoted by heartless and unscrupulous businessmen for the benefit of crooked gamblers and mobsters.

Luckily for the young Jackson he was spotted by the famous entertainer Al Jolson, who prompted Eddie Mead, a prominent manager, to take the precociously talented boxer under his wing. Henry changed his surname to Armstrong to conceal his ignominious history as a 'paid' fighter and achieved immediate success.

1937 was a busy year for Armstrong. He had no less than twenty-seven fights, winning all but one of them inside the distance. During this unparalleled run of victories he defeated Mike Belloise, who, as the New York Athletic Association's featherweight champion, also claimed he was the world title holder. In October the same year Armstrong put paid to any arguments over who was the genuine world featherweight champion when he knocked out Petey Sarron in six rounds on October 29 in New York.

In May the following year Armstrong gained his second world title when he outpointed the great Barney Ross to become the welterweight king. Ever ambitious, he then sought the lightweight crown, and in the summer of 1938 he beat Lou Ambers on points

BORN COLUMBUS, MISSISSIPPI, DECEMBER 12 1912 **TURNED PROFESSIONAL** 1931 **WORLD FEATHERWEIGHT CHAMPION** 1937–1938 **WORLD LIGHTWEIGHT CHAMPION** 1938–1939 **WORLD WELTERWEIGHT CHAMPION** 1938–1940 **WORLD CHAMPIONSHIP FIGHTS** (FEATHERWEIGHT) WON 1 (WELTERWEIGHT) WON 20, LOST 2 (LIGHTWEIGHT) WON 1, LOST 1 (MIDDLEWEIGHT) DREW 1 **DIED** LOS ANGELES, OCTOBER 23 1988

in a bitterly-fought fifteen-round contest held at Madison Square Garden, New York.

Finding it difficult to make the weight he gave up his featherweight title, and on August 22 1939 he also lost his lightweight crown in another savage struggle with Lou Ambers. However, he successfully defended his welterweight title nineteen times, and in March 1940 he very nearly collected his fourth world championship when he drew with the reigning middleweight title holder, Ceferino Garcia.

In October 1940, Armstrong finally met his match in the shape of Fritzie Zivic, who outpointed him in fifteen rounds to take away his welterweight title. In a return match the following year, Zivic confirmed his superiority over the slowing Armstrong by pummelling him to a twelve-round knockout defeat in New York.

Armstrong announced his retirement after the second Zivic fight but he was back in the ring only eighteen months later. By this time, though, he was past his best, but even so he did not finally quit the ring until 1945.

Henry Armstrong is the only person in history to hold three world titles simultaneously, and in an era when there were fewer weight divisions than there are now, and consequently much greater competition, that says a lot for the man who was dubbed 'Homicide Hank'. He had an abnormally slow heartbeat which enabled him to go flat out for fifteen rounds without tiring, and he used to flail away with his fists non-stop.

Tragically, Armstrong went into a sorry decline in his retirement. Always one for the women and the good life, he frittered away the vast fortune he had earned in the ring and became addicted to drugs and alcohol. He was ordained a Baptist minister in 1951 and changed his ways, but when he died he was blind and living in abject poverty.

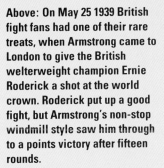

Above: On May 25 1939 British fight fans had one of their rare treats, when Armstrong came to London to give the British welterweight champion Ernie Roderick a shot at the world crown. Roderick put up a good fight, but Armstrong's non-stop windmill style saw him through to a points victory after fifteen rounds.

Right: Having taken the world featherweight championship away from Petey Sarron in October 1937, Armstrong went up a weight to challenge the superb Barney Ross for the welterweight crown on May 31 1938. Armstrong came through with a fifteen-round points victory at the Garden Bowl, Long Island City.

Top: Armstrong became the first boxer to hold three crowns at three different weights simultaneously when, at Madison Square Garden on the night of August 17 1938, he defeated the great Lou Ambers on points over fifteen rounds to take the lightweight championship.

Above: Armstrong fought hundreds of bouts but encountered only one boxer to whom he had to acknowledge true superiority. That was Fritzie Zivic, who defeated the champ twice at the end of his career.

TONY ZALE

Tony Zale, of Polish descent, came out of the steel mills of Gary, Indiana sixty-five years ago to tread a hard path to the middleweight championship. He was recognized by the NBA by virtue of a stoppage win over a durable, Seattle-based Czech called Al Hostak. This took place just before America entered the Second World War. Zale had previously outpointed Hostak in Chicago but it wasn't for the title. That fight came later and Tony had to win it in the champion's backyard. Taking no chances of losing a home-town points decision, he smashed Al to defeat in thirteen torrid rounds. Then, to prove he was no fluke champ, Tony knocked out Hostak in two rounds in 1941 and won the undisputed crown by trimming the consistent Georgie Abrams. The war came at a time when Zale was poised to cash in on the title, but the ensuing inactivity took his name off the sporting pages. He was in the US Navy for four years and his only ring activity during that period was in February 1942 when he lost to Billy Conn who was a light-heavy-weight bound for greatness. Tony's middleweight title was then frozen for the duration.

Returning in 1946, he had to start all over again to put himself in the public eye. Not one of his post-war fights went the distance. They were all exciting, and four of them produced some of the most dramatic and heavy punching moments of all time.

Zale was appropriately nicknamed 'The Man of Steel' and he lived up to that moniker in thrilling battles with Rocky Graziano and Marcel Cerdan. He was tough and had an abundance of what the old bare-knuckle fighters called 'bottom'. Even in the loneliest moment of his ring career, when he lost his title to Marcel Cerdan in his last fight, he refused to give up. When he could no longer stand, it was his cornermen who pulled him out of the fight. Zale was then past his thirty-fifth birthday and had been battling

BORN GARY, INDIANA, MAY 29 1913
TURNED PROFESSIONAL 1934
WORLD MIDDLEWEIGHT CHAMPION
1940–1941 (NBA RECOGNITION) 1941–1947 and 1948
WORLD CHAMPIONSHIP FIGHTS WON 5, LOST 2
DIED MARCH 21 1997

since 1934. He'd been a champion, on and off, for eight years and had always put up a stirring fight.

He was a prodigious puncher and won over half his fights by the short route, but in contrast to many other heavy hitters, Tony could take a hard dig too. He was disparaging of fighters with 'glass jaws' and remarked that their problem often stemmed from having a 'glass' heart. He spoke from a position of authority. In his fights with Rocky Graziano punishment was meted out on both sides, and it was the type that would have finished lesser men, but both went on to fight further tough battles. There is good film footage of the last of their three ring battles in which Zale boxed and hit with deadly precision. It is a gruelling film not suitable for the faint-hearted. The final blows, a right to the heart followed by a left hook to the jaw, still send a chill down the spine. Those three fights were ring wars. Zale won the first when he came back after a solid and merciless beating to knock his man out in the sixth round. It took the same time for Graziano to win the return, but this time he was being lambasted before he found an opening and shot over a chilling punch that left Tony defenceless. It should be recorded that Zale was never off his feet. We are dealing with an exceptionally hard and durable man and, as the final fight of this series was to show, a pin-point accurate, deadly hitter. It is a sad fact that films of the first two Zale v Graziano fights do not exist.

Tony Zale drew on all his reserves of stamina and courage in his last fight. From the start it was Cerdan's night, but he pummelled the champion and never scored a knockdown until the bell ended the twelfth round. Zale, who had withstood a steady thrashing valiantly, had grown old overnight, was too exhausted to get to his corner and slumped to his knees. He had thrown his last punch and fought no more, but if ever a

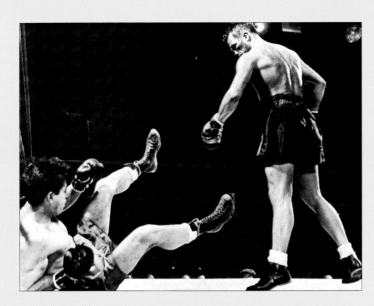

Above: This is the first of Zale's three-fight series with Rocky Graziano. Zale took a terrible beating for five rounds, then turned the tables to beat Rocky in the sixth.

Below: Zale's career comes to an end as he succumbs to France's Marcel Cerdan.

man went out on his shield it was the 'Man of Steel' from Gary, Indiana. He had been pivotal in reviving the post-war interest in boxing and had participated in four of the greatest middleweight fights. As his old opponent Graziano once put it: "Some fighter this Zale. Any other guy would be dead after taking what I dished out".

Zale fought another valiant battle in his later years when an implacable illness forced him into a wheelchair, but he took it all with the same courage that he showed in eighty-seven ring battles. He was eighty-three when he took the full count.

Above: Tony Zale was an outstanding champion. His three fights against Rocky Graziano contained some of the hardest hitting ever seen amongst middleweights.

JERSEY JOE WALCOTT

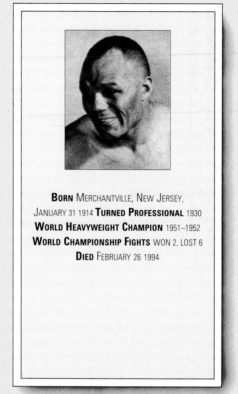

BORN MERCHANTVILLE, NEW JERSEY,
JANUARY 31 1914 **TURNED PROFESSIONAL** 1930
WORLD HEAVYWEIGHT CHAMPION 1951–1952
WORLD CHAMPIONSHIP FIGHTS WON 2, LOST 6
DIED FEBRUARY 26 1994

Until evergreen George Foreman came from behind to score that marvellous knockout win over Michael Moorer in 1994 at Las Vegas, Jersey Joe Walcott held the record of being the oldest man ever to win the premier prize in boxing, the Heavy-weight Championship of the World. Joe was thirty-seven having his fifth shot at the title and was in there with a man who had beaten him twice. He'd also lost two challenges to the great Joe Louis, but most people, including the fight's referee Ruby Goldstein, had Walcott a winner. Two of the judges voted for the champion and Jersey Joe, already an old campaigner, had to wait patiently for another three years and four defeats before his big moment arrived.

Does all this qualify Walcott for inclusion in the role-call of great fighters? Doubtfully – but his subsequent defeat in which he lost his title to Rocky Marciano was one of the division's hardest fights and Jersey Joe's remarkable performance, his punching ability, his tactical expertise and copybook boxing showed what had been denied to the boxing world during those long years when he was a younger man and in the wilderness: when he was too good for aspiring contenders, when he was forced to take fights when unfit and had to carry his opponent because a decisive win would have put him in the 'too dangerous, do not touch' category.

He floored Joe Louis in their first fight and did it again in the return, but chose to slug it out, and even at that late stage of Louis's career, you couldn't get away with it. All the slick footwork, the accurate counterpunching, the feinting, shuffling and solid hitting came to nothing once Louis got Walcott in his sights. Everyone thought that it was the last they would see of Jersey Joe as a title challenger, but he was still fighting for the title two years after Louis's last fight.

Born Arnold Raymond Cream in 1914, Joe started boxing for pay at the age of sixteen. His early record is obscure, with many gaps still to be filled in, but it does reveal that he was able to beat some very good men over the years and that he quit and came back so often that promoters lost sight of him. Joe said that at one time, when jobs were scarce, he was so hungry that he accepted a fight when he just could not stand up to body punishment

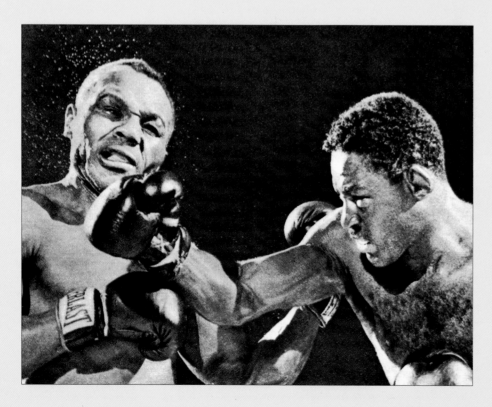

Left: Walcott takes a solid right from Ezzard Charles. They met four times with two wins each. The most important was in 1951 when Joe knocked out Ezzard and won the championship at age thirty-seven.

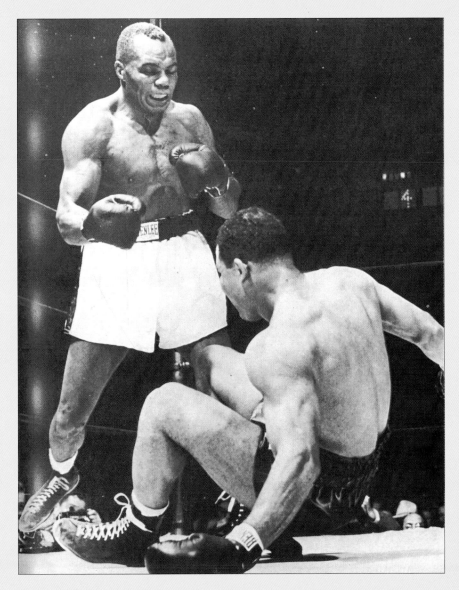

Left: Walcott put Joe Louis down in both their fights but couldn't keep him there.

Below: Jersey Joe Walcott, a tricky, switch-hitting and crafty campaigner who got his best opportunities late in his career.

and a punch to the ribs knocked him out. He represented the kind of boxer who was really too good and who was avoided unless he took it easy.

Things started to improve when Felix Bocchiccio took over as his manager in 1945. Boxing was enjoying a boom in those immediate post-war years. Suddenly regular fights were available. Between 1939 and the time that Bocchiccio held the reins, there are just seven entries on Walcott's fight ledger. He had more than that in the first ten months of 1945 and scored three notable wins: one on points over Joe Baksi and two stoppages against Curtis Sheppard and Lee Q Murray. Joe was now a contender but not a contender that top promoter Mike Jacobs wanted to know about. Jacobs steered the course of Joe Louis and Walcott had to get in line behind Billy Conn and Tami Mauriello. Even after Mauriello failed to dislodge Louis, Walcott still had to wait a couple of years before his chance came.

He was old and considered past his prime but old Jersey Joe had only just begun to fight with the wraps off. He had nothing to lose and everything to gain and showed respect but no fear when faced by one of the very great heavyweight champions. Louis, believing he had lost the title, left the ring before the decision was announced, but it went into the annals of fistiana as a win, and four years were to pass before Walcott hung one of boxing's deadliest left hooks on Ezzard Charles's jaw to become champion. It is often forgotten that he outpointed Charles in the return match because he was beaten by Marciano in his next fight, but fifty years after that titanic encounter with Rocky, the video film of it is still inspiring. Joe earned his place among the greats. That film, and the memory of the left hook that separated Ezzard Charles from his senses and from his title, is all the evidence required to put Walcott in the Hall of Fame.

JOE LOUIS

Christened Joseph Louis Barrow, the 'Brown Bomber', as he became known, was born into a poverty-stricken family in the deep South of the United States. His family moved to Detroit when he was ten and it was there that he learned to box while he should have been attending his violin lessons. After winning the Golden Gloves award for light-heavyweights in 1934 he turned professional, and proceeded to win twelve contests within a year. His reputation spread far and wide and in June 1935 he fought the former heavyweight champion, Primo Carnera, at Yankee Stadium before a crowd of 62,000 people. Carnera lasted just six rounds.

Three months after the Carnera fight, Louis tackled another former champion, Max Baer, who managed to last for just four rounds. It seemed as if nothing could stop the budding champion, until in 1936 Max Schmeling felled him, and he was counted out in the twelfth round of their contest.

Louis captured the world heavyweight crown in Chicago in 1937, when he knocked out James J

BORN LEXINGTON, ALABAMA, MAY 13 1914 **TURNED PROFESSIONAL** 1934 **WORLD HEAVYWEIGHT CHAMPION** 1937–1949 **TITLE BOUTS** WON 27, LOST 1 **DIED** LAS VEGAS, APRIL 12 1981

Braddock in eight rounds. Two months after winning the title he defended it against the Welshman, Tommy Farr. Louis won, but Farr became one of relatively few men ever to go the distance with the 'Brown Bomber'. After the Farr fight, Louis took on fighters at regular intervals in what came to be called his 'Bum of the Month' campaign. But his victories were against quality fighters as well, including solid professionals such as Arturo Godoy and Bob Pastor. A particularly satisfying victory for Louis was a return match against Max Schmeling, who was pulverized to an emphatic and humiliating defeat in two minutes four seconds.

In 1942 Louis joined the United States Army as a physical education instructor, but he returned to the ring in 1946. He defended his title four more times, including two bouts with 'Jersey' Joe Walcott, and then retired, undefeated, in 1949. However, pressure from the taxman forced Louis out of retirement a year later and he attempted to regain the championship from Ezzard Charles. By this time, the 'Brown

Right: Tommy Farr put up an extraordinary show against Louis when they met in New York City on August 30 1937. He was desperately unlucky to meet the new champion on his first defence – and the 'Brown Bomber' was in his prime. Even so, Farr was no 'Bum of the Month', and many critics, not only from the British Isles, considered that the fifteen-round points decision might have justifiably gone the other way under different circumstances.

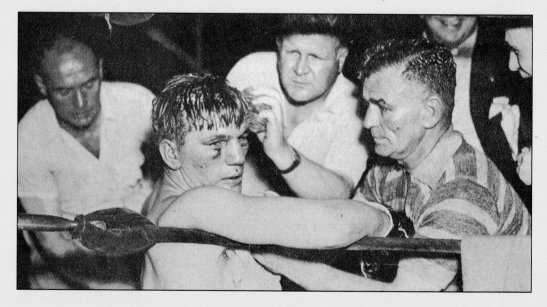

Left: Every decade or so there comes along a fighter who is so good, and so much better than the opposition, that the public comes to believe that he can never be beaten. In later years, Marciano was such a figure, and Ali and Tyson after him. But of all the greats in boxing's record books, it is difficult to think of a fighter who dominated his age to the extent that Louis ruled the twelve-year period from June 22 1937 to March 1 1949.

Below: Louis lost only three times: once, to Schmeling, on the way up; and then to Ezzard Charles and Marciano during an ill-conceived come-back. Schmeling must have regretted defeating the young 'Brown Bomber': when he later met a more mature Louis for the title, he took just about the worst beating in ring history, and is seen here going down in the first.

Bomber' was a shadow of his former self and he lost his twenty-seventh championship fight on points. Tragically, Louis' attempted comeback did not end there. He went on to have a fight against the rising Rocky Marciano in 1951: he was knocked through the ropes and the fight was stopped in the eighth round.

In his career Louis defended his title more times than any other heavyweight in history, and he succeeded in knocking out five former world champions. His style in the ring was deceptive. His footwork could look slow and ponderous, but the speed with which he delivered his power-laden punches was formidable, and few men could stand up to one of his onslaughts. He also took good care of his body and never appeared in the ring out of prime condition.

Despite winning some $5 million in his career as a boxer, Louis was perpetually in financial trouble, and when his boxing days were finally over he was obliged to earn his living as a casino host in Las Vegas. Whatever his later circumstances he will always remain a legendary figure in boxing, and he was a fine sportsman in every sense of the word.

Left: 'Jersey' Joe Walcott was a great rival to Louis. In their first meeting on December 5 1947, the referee voted a victory to Walcott, but the two judges went against him to leave Louis the crown. Louis left no room for doubt with an eleven-round KO in the return match six months later.

MARCEL CERDAN

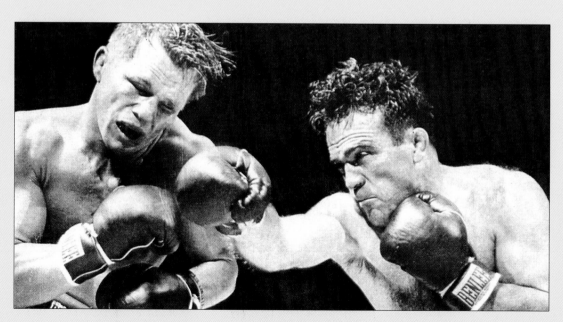

BORN SIDI-BEL-ABBES, ALGERIA, JULY 22 1916
TURNED PROFESSIONAL 1934
WORLD MIDDLEWEIGHT CHAMPION 1948–1949
WORLD CHAMPIONSHIP FIGHTS WON 1, LOST 1
DIED OCTOBER 27 1949

Marcel Cerdan, born in French-occupied Algeria in 1916, was one of the greatest fighters ever to come out of France, and was certainly the most popular of her fighting sons since Georges Carpentier graced Parisian rings at the time that the First World War was brewing. When the New York-bound plane in which he and manager Jo Longman were travelling crashed into a mountain peak in the Azores, it was not only the French who mourned. Cerdan – and his manager – were also idolized in America, England and the rest of Europe.

They were en route to the United States with the intention of regaining the world middleweight title that Marcel had controversially lost to Jake LaMotta four months previously. A shoulder injury incurred early in the fight left Cerdan to battle on with one effective arm. His left was not even of moderate use for defensive purposes. Cerdan was incredibly tough. He took his punishment without losing his feet and rejected his cornermen's advice to quit until his cause was so obviously lost and he could take no more. At the bell

for the tenth round he stayed in his corner. Nobody could have known that this was his last fight and that his life-clock was clicking away.

He was a brilliant middleweight – hard punching, immensely strong, a sound tactician and apart from a couple of disqualification losses, he beat every man he fought....with the exception of LaMotta, of course. If he had been given the opportunity to avenge that loss, then his next challenger would have been Sugar Ray Robinson. Can you imagine what a wonderful fight that would have been? In the eyes of many, Robinson was the greatest fighter of the twentieth century, but he had difficulty with men of Cerdan's style. Marcel Cerdan had a long career that began in 1934 with just one year of inactivity (because of the conflict in Europe between 1939 and 1945). He cleaned up all the opposition in France, Belgium, Italy and North Africa, and once the war was over he set his sights on the United States. He'd been boxing for fourteen years, so this was not a case of being fed to the lions. He got a very hard test in his American

Right: Cerdan (right) on the way to the middleweight title via a twelve round win over defending champion Tony Zale, who is shown here taking a heavy right.

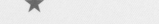

Above: The weigh-in for the championship fight with Tony Zale.

Above: Cerdan shown reading the New York Daily News on the morning after his triumph over Tony Zale.

Left: Marcel Cerdan, a formidable fighter.

debut but clearly beat George Abrams, then knocked out Harold Green and ruined the highly touted Lavern Roach who was never a force again. Tony Zale, the world title-holder, was to follow the same path six months later, but first of all the Frenchman returned home to defend his European title. He lost this in Brussels to the local hero Cyrille Delannoit but it was a shocking home-town decision and Cerdan got his revenge two months later. He insisted on going back to Brussels to achieve it!

That first controversial loss had a ray of sunshine to it. In America, Tony Zale figured that Cerdan would be a safe title defence. He would have lost much of his confidence if he'd seen his challenger reverse the Delannoit loss but even so, Zale was a great champion too and he stood up to a steady and savage hammering from Cerdan before succumbing at the end of the twelfth round. Marcel returned home in triumph and to the adulation of his fans. Rather than rest on his laurels,

he impressively knocked out British champion Dick Turpin in London's Earls Court and then returned to the country of his birth to dish out the same medicine, but in less time, to the very useful Polish scrapper, Lucien Krawczyk who held a victory over Kid Tunero.

The LaMotta fight followed and the surprise result, in what was considered to be a routine defence of the title, caused the most intense and determined spell of preparation of Cerdan's long career. He was obsessed with the desire to regain his championship not only for his own sake: he was very loyal to his huge army of fans. Newspapers were printing previews, tickets were selling fast, but Air France flight FBA 21 changed the course of boxing history when it took the life of France's greatest post-war fighter. A day of mourning was ordered, but the tide of grief spread far beyond the shores of France.

ARCHIE MOORE

Archie Moore, whose original name was Archibald Lee Wright, had one of the most bizarre careers in boxing history. For a start, there is some confusion over his exact birth date: in his boxing days *he* maintained that he was born in 1916, while his *mother* said he was born in 1913. Whatever the case, he became champion extremely late, having boxed professionally for over fifteen years before winning his first crown, the world light-heavyweight title.

At the age of sixteen he was a welterweight, but he proceeded to gain in bulk as the years went by and he ultimately challenged for the world heavyweight title. One reason for his slow rise to the top was the fact that he had an extraordinary number of managers in his career, eight in all. Moore was acutely aware that managers frequently took advantage of black boxers at the time, so, possessing a fiery personality, he swapped managers as soon as he had any suspicion, however unfounded, that he was being exploited.

'Ageless Archie' had such a reputation as a knockout specialist during the late 1940s that champions were reluctant to fight him. Finally he teamed up with the extraordinary Jack 'Doc' Kearns, who eventually got him a fight against Joey Maxim for the world light-heavyweight title in 1952. The bout was held at St Louis and Moore won the fifteen-round contest on points. Over the next two years he had two return matches with Maxim and on each occasion he outpointed the challenger over the full fifteen rounds.

Moore defended his light-heavyweight title seven more times, winning on each occasion. However, there were some close calls. In 1956 he fought the West Indian Yolande Pompey in London. The fight turned into a yawn and in the ninth round the referee told the boxers that he was going to disqualify the contest

BORN BENOIT, MISSISSIPPI,
DECEMBER 13 1916
TURNED PROFESSIONAL 1935
WORLD LIGHT-HEAVYWEIGHT
CHAMPION 1952–1962
WORLD CHAMPIONSHIP FIGHTS
(LIGHT-HEAVYWEIGHT) WON 9
(HEAVYWEIGHT) LOST 2
DIED SAN DIEGO, DECEMBER 9 1998

unless they started to fight. Responding to the threat, Moore came out like a whirlwind in the tenth round and knocked out the hapless Pompey.

In 1958 he travelled to Montreal to face the Canadian, Yvon Durelle. The challenger had the champion on the floor three times in the opening round but Moore came back to win by a knockout in the eleventh.

During his career Moore made two challenges for the world heavyweight title. The first was against Rocky Marciano in New York in 1955. He floored Marciano in the second round, but eventually came off second best and was knocked out in nine rounds. A year later he challenged Floyd Patterson for the vacant heavyweight title, but came to grief in five rounds.

In 1960 the National Boxing Association stripped him of his light-heavyweight title for 'inactivity', but he was still considered the champion by other boxing authorities and made his final defence in 1961, outpointing Giulio Rinaldi.

After the Rinaldi conquest, Moore's world title was taken away from him by all the boxing authorities but he still continued to fight, mainly as a heavyweight. He took on the budding Cassius Clay in 1962, being knocked out in the fourth round, and the following year he finally decided to hang up his gloves for good.

In his career Moore succeeded in knocking out no less than 145 opponents. His technique was to soften up his man with an unrelenting stream of blows before moving in for the *coup de grâce*. He is remembered for his outrageous publicity gimmicks, as well as for his boxing skills. He secured his fight with Marciano only after writing to every sports editor in the United States and having posters made up showing Marciano as a wanted man and himself as a sheriff.

Above: Archie was a great light-heavyweight champion, but his two shots at moving up to challenge for the world heavyweight crown both ended in disaster. In the first, his historic clash with Marciano, Moore is seen on the canvas in the ninth, with referee Harry Kessler counting him out. This was Marciano's last defence before retiring undefeated. Moore immediately challenged Floyd Patterson for the vacant title, but was KO'd in five on November 30 1956. Below: Canadian challenger Yvon Durelle.

Above and left: Archie Moore was an all-time great, both as boxer and as ring character. He was over thirty-five years of age when he won his first world title by taking the light-heavyweight crown from Joey Maxim on points over fifteen rounds on December 17 1952. He held that title until it was finally stripped from him on the grounds of inactivity in February 1962.

PETER KANE

BORN GOLBORNE, LANCASHIRE, FEBRUARY 28 1918
TURNED PROFESSIONAL 1934
WORLD FLYWEIGHT CHAMPION 1938–1943
WORLD CHAMPIONSHIP FIGHTS WON 1, LOST 2
DIED JULY 21 1991

Few boxers who were at their peak form prior to World War II managed to continue where they had left off once peace was declared. One who did was Peter Kane, who went up to the bantamweight division after hostilities had ceased, but whose flyweight career had reached its apogee in 1938 when he beat America's Jackie Jurich for the vacant title. In June of that same year, Benny Lynch, the greatest fighter ever to come out of Scotland, held the title. Benny had a water-retention problem because of previously undiagnosed alcoholism. When defending against Jurich, whom he knocked out, Benny couldn't even make the bantamweight limit and forfeited his title on the scales. Kane then beat Jurich for the vacant title. He had drawn with Lynch in a World and British title challenge the previous March. That was the last flyweight fight in which Lynch retained a semblance of his greatness – and great he most definitely was. In his prime, Lynch had stopped Kane in thirteen rounds after scoring a first round knockdown with a terrific punch. That Peter came back to compete on even terms, and then forced a draw in his next fight with the champion, speaks volumes for his fighting qualities, but that is getting too far ahead of the story.

Kane followed a remarkable path to the championship. He was boxing for pay at seventeen and, apart from the loss to Lynch, had cleared up the field by the time he was twenty. The cream of European flyweights faced him on the way and they all went home beaten. This is some achievement when you consider the excellent quality of the available opposition. As a teenager, Peter beat Frank Bonsor, Jimmy Stewart, Praxille Gyde, Petit Biquet, Pat Warburton, Jimmy Warnock and Enrico Urbinati. None of these lasted the distance – Peter was a very hard puncher. Valentin Angelmann was unique in that he twice went the twelve round course, but up to the start of the war in September 1939, of Peter's 59 fights there was one draw (Lynch) and only sixteen distance fights. This leaves a remarkably high percentage of knockout victories.

The war years brought a couple of defeats to mar his winning streak, but they were rather meaningless under the circumstances, until the one that created a record Peter would rather not have achieved.

Left: Kane beats Baltazar Sangchilli of Spain in 1939. Before he was 20, Peter had beaten the cream of continental Europe's flyweights and bantamweights.

Left: Peter Kane, receiving the plaudits of the pressmen after beating Theo Medina for the European Bantamweight Championship. On his right is Nel Tarleton, former British Featherweight Champion. Kane had scored his second win over Medina and had well and truly come back after his career went into limbo during the war.

In 1943, with fistic activity slowing down, Jackie Paterson took his title with a first round knockout win that is still the quickest in the division's history. Sixty-one seconds is all it took to relegate Peter to the rank of ex-champion. He had three more wins and hung up his gloves until the war was over.

Three years' inactivity put a few pounds on his frame. He returned to the fray in 1946 and ran up five more wins, and then beat Ireland's Bunty Doran. This served notice that he was still a force to be reckoned with, and when he stopped the European Bantamweight champion Theo Medina, in a non-title meeting in Manchester, he consolidated his claims for a crack at the title. Peter was a class act though. When challenged by Hawaiian Dado Marino he accepted and boxed brilliantly to win on points. Dado had just beaten Rinty Monaghan, who was to become world flyweight title holder before the year was over, and later on Marino

won the title himself. It was a dangerous fight to take with a shot at Medina in the offing, but Kane could have given any man in the world a good fight, and he went into the European Bantamweight title challenge with an air of confidence. The record books show that Peter won the title but they do not show what a fine fight and what a great victory it was. He was nearly thirty and he never rose to those heights again. He may have been unlucky to lose his title a year later to Guido Ferracin, but it cannot be disputed that the Italian was the better man in the return match. Cuts are what stopped Peter but he had difficulty in making the weight and was slower throughout. A following points loss to Stan Rowan convinced him that it was time for a long, distinguished career to come to a close.

He lived until he was seventy-three, but a car accident in his late sixties did much to hasten his death. He was one of the best 110-pound men ever to grace a boxing ring.

FREDDIE MILLS

Freddie Mills is famed for being one of the most recklessly brave fighters ever to have entered a ring. As a young teenager, he worked as a milkman, boxing as an amateur in his spare time. He took the hard route to boxing stardom by becoming a professional fighter in a fairground booth in which he took on all-comers, in all their various shapes and sizes. While still a booth fighter, he met the former British lightweight champion, Gypsy Daniels, who encouraged his endeavours and passed on much of his hard-earned experience.

Mills first rose to national prominence when he outpointed the able middleweight Jock McAvoy over ten rounds in August 1940. A return fight resulted in McAvoy being hurt and stopped in the opening round. This led to a contest against the British and Empire champion, Len Harvey, who also held the British Boxing Board of Control's version of the world championship. Harvey was

BORN PARKSTONE, DORSET, JUNE 26 1919
TURNED PROFESSIONAL 1936 **WORLD LIGHT-HEAVYWEIGHT CHAMPION** 1946–1950 **WORLD CHAMPIONSHIP FIGHTS** WON 1, LOST 2 **DIED** LONDON, JULY 25 1965

knocked out of the ring in the second round and was unable to climb back to beat the count.

Service in the RAF during World War Two deprived Mills of some of his best years, and in 1946 his rustiness showed when he was stopped in ten rounds by the American holder of the world light-heavyweight championship, Gus Lesnevich. In the same year he rashly accepted an offer to fight the heavyweight, Joe Baksi, who was some twenty-five pounds heavier than himself. The inevitable happened, and Mills was stopped in six rounds.

Slipping back to the light-heavyweight division, Mills had a return fight against Lesnevich in 1948 and this time he came out on top, winning the fifteen-round contest in London on points. However, Mills was determined to emulate his boyhood hero, Jack Dempsey, and again challenged the heavyweights. He beat the South African champion, Johnny Ralph, in eight rounds, but his attempt to wrest the British and Empire heavyweight titles from Bruce Woodcock in 1949 was thwarted when he was stopped in the fourteenth round.

Mills had his last fight in 1950 when he faced the American, Joey Maxim, in London with his world light-heavyweight title at stake. The Englishman fought as bravely as ever but he was weary after his tussles with heavyweights and he was counted out in the tenth round. For Mills it meant more than just the loss of his world title, as several of his teeth went missing as well.

Deciding that he had had enough, Mills announced his retirement immediately after losing to Maxim and invested his considerable earnings in a restaurant. He also became a hugely popular radio and television personality, but, despite his cheerful demeanour, he was persistently troubled by personal and financial troubles. His life came to a horrific and

Left: The superb American light-heavyweight, Gus Lesnevich. During the 1940s, after Billy Conn had given up the crown in 1941 to challenge Louis as a heavyweight, the light-heavyweight class became highly confused, with no clear succession. Things were further complicated by the war, which effectively ruled out the British and European fighters. Most authorities recognized Lesnevich as the champion, a position he confirmed by defeating Mills in 1946. But Mills was out-of-shape because of years of inactivity during his war service, and triumphed two years later when he beat Lesnevich in London to take the world title.

Left: Mills ranks alongside Henry Cooper as the most popular boxing hero of the British public. Sophistication and artistry were in small supply, but he had enough courage and fighting spirit for a man twice his size. His 1946 encounter with Lesnevich ranks as one of the bravest British boxing performances of all time. Mills had just been demobbed, having been ill in the Far East during the last part of the war. He found himself in the ring with a fight-hardened pro, who happened also to be one of the best light-heavyweights in history. For ten rounds the two men slugged it out in a frightening barrage, and it was only when Mills went down three times in the tenth that the referee saw sense and stopped the fight.

Left: Like Mickey Walker, Freddie Mills was a fearless fighter who constantly chose to mix it with the heavyweights, never knowing when he was beaten. He is seen here taking his second defeat from British heavyweight champion Bruce Woodcock in 1949.

tragic end as a result of a gunshot wound. He was found dead in his car, and although the verdict was that he had committed suicide, his sad demise still remains something of a mystery. He will always be remembered for his quite remarkable courage.

Above: Joey Maxim took Mills' world title on January 24 1950, stopping the champ in a ten-round encounter. Maxim lost the crown to Archie Moore in 1952.

'SUGAR' RAY ROBINSON

'**S**ugar' Ray Robinson was christened Walker Smith and he did not adopt his 'stage' name until he turned professional. His mother and sisters moved from Detroit to a poor region of New York when he was a young lad, and he was obliged to keep the family by tap-dancing on the sidewalks. His great passion, however, was for boxing, and he worshipped the great heavyweight Joe Louis.

He had immense success as an amateur, winning eighty-five bouts, forty of them in the first round. He crowned his amateur career by winning Golden Gloves titles in the featherweight and lightweight divisions and elected to turn professional in 1940.

According to legend, he was substituted for a fighter by the name of Ray Robinson on his professional début and was so entranced by the other man's name that he decided to keep it. Later someone told his manager, George Gainford, that he had a sweet mover in his stable and Gainford is reputed to have answered, 'Yes, he's as sweet as sugar.' The name was complete and stuck with him.

'Sugar' Ray had unparalleled success in his first years as a professional, winning forty successive contests before losing to Jake LaMotta. In all Robinson fought LaMotta six times, and this was the only one of those six fights he lost. In 1946 he challenged Tommy Bell for the vacant welterweight world title and won on points. He went on to defend the title successfully five times before relinquishing it, reluctantly, on beating his old adversary LaMotta for the middleweight crown in 1951.

As the new middleweight champion Robinson toured Europe in 1951 complete with a veritable army of assistants and trainers, and accepted an offer from the promoter Jack Solomons to defend his title

BORN DETROIT, MICHIGAN, MAY 3 1921
TURNED PROFESSIONAL 1940 **WORLD WELTERWEIGHT CHAMPION** 1946–1951
WORLD MIDDLEWEIGHT CHAMPION 1951–1960 **WORLD CHAMPIONSHIP FIGHTS**
(WELTERWEIGHT) WON 6 (MIDDLEWEIGHT) WON 8, LOST 6, DREW 1 (LIGHT-HEAVYWEIGHT) LOST 1 **DIED** LOS ANGELES, APRIL 12 1989

against Randolph Turpin. Over-confident and arrogant, Robinson under-estimated Turpin and lost the bout on a points decision. Turpin, however, did not have a grasp on the title for very long: sixty-four days later Robinson won it back at a contest held at the New York Polo Grounds before an audience of some 61,000 people.

The following year Robinson saw off the challenges of Carl 'Bobo' Olson and Rocky Graziano for the middleweight championship, and he then had the audacity to challenge Joey Maxim for the light-heavyweight title. Robinson drew ahead on points, but he failed to come out of his corner for the fourteenth round. It is true to say that he was beaten by the heat rather than his opponent; the atmosphere was so close that the referee had already collapsed in the tenth round and had been replaced.

Robinson announced his retirement soon after his fight with Maxim, but he returned to the ring in 1955 and regained the middleweight title after knocking out the usurper, Olson, in two rounds. He lost the title to Gene Fullmer in January 1957, but gained his revenge five months later by knocking Fullmer out in five rounds. Carmen Basilio took the title from him in 1957 but, never one to give up, he became a champion for the fifth time when he beat Basilio on points in a rematch in 1958. He finally lost the middleweight title for the last time when Paul Pender beat him in 1960. He challenged for the undisputed title one more time, and for the NBA version twice more, but finally gave up his ring career on December 10 1965 at a retirement party.

One of the most stylish and punishing boxers of all time, Robinson had an extravagant lifestyle that endeared him to the gossip columnists. Sadly he died of Alzheimer's disease in 1989.

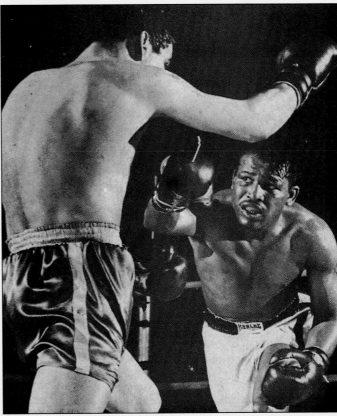

Above: A thirty-four-year-old Robinson comes out of retirement to despatch 'Bobo' Olson in two and take the middleweight title for the third time.

Left: One of the true legends of the ring, Robinson came out of retirement on countless occasions, and won the middleweight crown five times.

Above and left: One of Robinson's last great flurries was against Carmen Basilio, a fine fighter with an old-time slugger's heart. Basilio took Robinson's title on September 23 1957 on a split decision: Robinson came back eight months later to beat Basilio and take the crown for the fifth time.

EZZARD CHARLES

Ezzard Charles has never really been forgiven by the American public for beating Joe Louis, and even Charles himself was sorry when he outpointed his hero. He was, however, a great boxer who deserves more recognition than he receives.

He rose to prominence as a teenager, winning all of his forty-two amateur contests including the middleweight Golden Gloves championship of 1939. Turning professional in 1940, he moved up to heavyweight in 1943 and had a run of success that earned him the nickname 'The Cincinnati Cobra'. In 1949, Joe Louis announced his retirement and the National Boxing Association pitted Charles and 'Jersey' Joe Walcott against each other to decide who should hold its world heavyweight title. The bout took place on June 22 1949 in Chicago, and Charles emerged the victor on points. To many

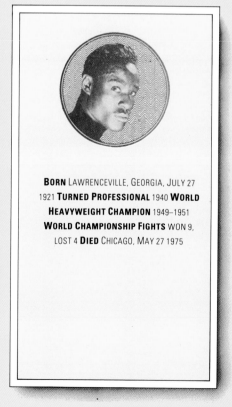

BORN LAWRENCEVILLE, GEORGIA, JULY 27 1921 **TURNED PROFESSIONAL** 1940 **WORLD HEAVYWEIGHT CHAMPION** 1949–1951 **WORLD CHAMPIONSHIP FIGHTS** WON 9, LOST 4 **DIED** CHICAGO, MAY 27 1975

people, however, Louis was still champion and consequently few people paid much attention to the new champion – despite the fact that he successfully defended his title three times, including once against Gus Lesnevich. In 1950, plagued by financial problems, Louis made a comeback and fought Charles for the world title in New York. Louis was by this time a shadow of the great boxer he had once been, and it was no surprise when Charles was proclaimed the points winner after fifteen rounds. Rather ridiculously, the public still refused to give Charles credit for his achievements.

In March 1951 Charles got the better of 'Jersey' Joe Walcott for the second time and in May he beat the talented Joey Maxim. In July the same year he had a third fight with his old adversary Walcott and this time he lost the title after

Below: Charles v Marciano in their still-remembered encounter of June 17 1954. At this time Marciano was a god of the ring; so supreme as to be considered invincible. He had won the world heavyweight title from Walcott on September 23 1952 on a knock-out, and every defence he made of his crown was also won inside the distance – except this first encounter with Charles. Despite his long and distinguished career, and his many championships and championship defences, it is thought by most critics that his performance in this points defeat by Marciano represented his finest hour.

Left and above: Charles' rivalry with 'Jersey' Joe Walcott was one of the greatest in ring history. They fought four times: Charles came out top in 1949, winning the vacant world crown, and in March 1951, in a title defence. Walcott took the title from him in July 1951, and successfully defended it against him in June 1952.

being knocked out in the seventh round. A fourth battle with Walcott a year later resulted in another defeat, and it seemed like the end of the road.

Two years later, however, he reappeared in the ring to challenge for the world title which was by this time held by Rocky Marciano. In their first fight, held in New York on June 17 1954, Charles used his wits and experience and boxed extremely cleverly. He was eventually well beaten on points, but he did at least earn the satisfaction of becoming the only challenger to take the 'Brockton Blockbuster' the distance. In a second battle with Marciano three months later, the thirty-three-year-old Charles put up another brave effort and badly hurt the champion's face, but it was not enough and he was knocked out in the eighth.

After his two tussles with Marciano Charles lost much of his fire but he refused to quit. It was a mistake, as he lost the majority of his later fights and gained few admirers. He finally decided to retire in September 1959.

Sadly Charles retired an embittered man, sickened that his talent was never fully appreciated. During his career he fought and beat many of the best heavyweights around – it was sheer bad luck that he emerged at a time when Joe Louis was revered as a national hero and favourite. It was also unfortunate that he should encounter Rocky Marciano when his own best boxing days were behind him.

ROCKY GRAZIANO

Rocky Graziano's championship record does not appear very impressive on paper, but in each and every fight he gave his all, and his approach to boxing so captured the imagination of the American public that he became a legendary figure like Jack Dempsey and John L Sullivan before him.

He was born Rocco Barbella, the son of poor Italian immigrants who lived in a desolate tenement block in the shabby East Side of New York. As a child all he knew was crime. He frequently absconded from school and roamed the streets with gangs that stole anything that wasn't actually cemented to the sidewalk. He was perpetually in trouble with the law and saw the insides of remand homes and detention centres on a regular basis. He was called up to join the United States Army but could not bow to authority and ended up in military prison. He was eventually dishonourably discharged from the army and, had he not taken up boxing, would almost certainly have become an irredeemable hoodlum. As it was he learned to vent his deep-seated hatred in the ring and he became a success as an amateur, winning a middleweight Golden Gloves title.

He had earlier changed his name to Graziano to conceal his unenviable past, and he turned professional when twenty. For four years he fought his way up until he was given a chance to wrest the middleweight world title from Tony Zale. Graziano and Zale met for the first time on September 27 1946 in New York. The fight was savage and neither man gave any quarter. Both men were knocked down in the first round, but Zale was the quicker to recover: he retained the title on knocking out Graziano in the sixth round.

The following year Zale and Graziano had a rematch in Chicago which was contested equally viciously. Zale appeared to be heading for victory as he merclessly slugged away, but the challenger dredged up all his reserves of courage and energy in the sixth round and produced a stunning counter-attack that ended with Zale hanging on the ropes.

With the public baying for more, a third championship contest between Graziano and Zale was arranged. The bout took place on June 10 1948 in Newark, New Jersey and Zale emerged triumphant, knocking out Graziano in the third round to reclaim the crown.

Four years elapsed before Graziano again challenged for the middleweight world title, which was by this time in the possession of 'Sugar' Ray Robinson. The fight, which took place in Chicago in 1952, was embarrassingly onesided. After knocking the champion down briefly in round one, Graziano proved no match for Robinson: the challenger was knocked out in three rounds.

Reluctant to retire, Graziano had one more fight after his defeat at Robinson's hands, but Chuck Davey outpointed him and this defeat finally convinced him that it was time to hang up the gloves.

Graziano could hardly be called a great technician or a clever boxer; when he fought, he fought for real and he was not concerned with the niceties of the game. He had phenomenal courage and determination and his three battles with Zale are among the bloodiest ever recorded. He enjoyed fighting men who had an explosive style similar to his own, but he was no match for anybody who was prepared to bide his time. However, his spirit and personality won him millions of admirers the world over.

Graziano's extraordinary career was retold in the book *Somebody Up There Likes Me*, which was later made into a film starring Paul Newman. He might have featured in the film himself, as he had considerable success in a second career as a screen actor.

BORN NEW YORK CITY, JANUARY 1 1922
TURNED PROFESSIONAL 1942 **WORLD MIDDLEWEIGHT CHAMPION** 1947–1948
WORLD CHAMPIONSHIP FIGHTS WON 1, LOST 3 **DIED** NEW YORK CITY, MAY 23 1990

Above and left: Graziano's name heads this page, but it might just as well be Zale's: the greatness of these two boxers comes not in their individual careers, but in their combined rivalry. Here Graziano (right of picture, on the scales) is seen at the weigh-in before his victory in the second fight of their epic series.

Above and right: Tony Zale defended his middleweight crown successfully against Graziano in 1946, but lost out to him in six rounds on July 16 1947 in Chicago. On June 10 1948, in one of the most keenly-anticipated fights ever, Zale KO'd Graziano in the third to prove to his own satisfaction that he was the better man.

JAKE LaMotta

BORN BRONX, NEW YORK, JULY 10 1922
TURNED PROFESSIONAL 1941 **WORLD**
MIDDLEWEIGHT CHAMPION 1949–1951
WORLD CHAMPIONSHIP FIGHTS WON 3,
LOST 1

Like his boyhood friend Rocky Graziano, Jake LaMotta was born and brought up in a run-down neighbourhood of New York and was destined to lead a life of crime until he was harnessed into a boxing career. Unlike Graziano, however, he never completely broke free from the criminal fraternity, and much of his career was blighted by powerful Mafia operators who manipulated his fights and his destiny.

A naturally aggressive man, LaMotta, whose original Christian name was Giacobe, saw boxing as an obvious way to earn a living. At the start of his career he shunned overtures made to him by mobsters and refused to be the hireling of a Mafia manager. However, organized crime virtually controlled boxing in New York at the time and the unfortunate LaMotta discovered that they could disrupt his career at will. For nine years he defied the gangsters and for nine years he fought without getting anywhere. During this period he had nearly one hundred bouts, many promoted by himself at his own venue (among his victims was a young 'Sugar' Ray Robinson). But the word was out from the mob, so promoters continued to look the other way until he finally succumbed to Mafia pressure and, for a considerable fee, was permitted to have a crack at the world middleweight title.

The champion at the time was an equally rugged fighter, Marcel Cerdan, and when they met in Detroit on June 16 1949 the Frenchman was the hot favourite. The fight was ferocious and in the third round Cerdan's arm was dislocated when LaMotta flung him to the canvas. The gallant champion fought on

Right: During his early career LaMotta refused to co-operate in the fight-fixing schemes of the criminal fraternity. As they virtually controlled boxing in New York, this left him with nowhere to go: no manager or promoter could afford to take an interest in him, so he had to set up his own contests against no-hope boxers in anonymous venues. In this 1943 slugfest he beat 'Sugar' Ray Robinson. At the time Robinson had won forty straight fights, and was contending for the championships. Such a victory should have set LaMotta up for the big-time, but his career continued to remain dormant for another six years.

Right: LaMotta could slug it out with the best, but had more problems against genuine ringcraft. He caught Robinson early in his career, and beat him; but the mature 'Sugar' Ray was a different matter. Robinson is seen here taking the crown by guilefully boxing 'The Bull' to defeat on Valentine's Day 1951.

Above left, and above right: LaMotta's big break came against the French slugger, Marcel Cerdan (above), at Briggs Stadium on June 16 1949. The European had taken the middleweight title from Tony Zale in 1948, and this was his first defence: he was heavily tipped to win. LaMotta came out like a bull, and mixed it from the start. The Frenchman damaged his arm in the third, when LaMotta threw him to the canvas: disabled, he soldiered on, but soaked up so much punishment that the fight was stopped in ten. LaMotta is seen (above left) celebrating his first title.

for six more rounds but failed to come out for the tenth – America had a new world champion.

LaMotta was contracted for a return fight against Cerdan but the Frenchman was killed in a plane crash. His new challenger was the Italian Tiberio Mitri, whom he outpointed over fifteen rounds in 1950. Another Frenchman, Laurent Dauthille, was coasting to a points victory in LaMotta's third defence when, with seconds to go in the last round, the champion flattened his opponent to retain the title.

'Sugar' Ray Robinson put an end to LaMotta's reign as middleweight champion of the world in February 1951 when, utilizing his immaculate technique, he stopped him in the thirteenth round. The former champion attempted a comeback, but after two defeats he lost his chance of having another title fight and he finally decided to retire in 1954.

After hanging up his gloves, LaMotta started a second career as a stand-up comedian with a modicum of success, but he led a turbulent and troubled life and was not exactly a quiet, contented man. He lived his life outside the ring rather like he did when in it: fiercely and to the limit. While he was fighting professionally, he earned the nickname 'The Bronx Bull', which was an apt description of his style: he crouched low and charged with both fists flailing.

The film of LaMotta's extraordinary life, *Raging Bull* (1980), starred Robert de Niro, and did much to bring the boxer back into the public eye. One of the tragedies of LaMotta's career was that he was never allowed to box world-class opposition while in his prime: by the time he was able to compete he was very nearly past his peak and had soaked up an astonishing amount of punishment.

WILLIE PEP

There will never be another featherweight to match the remarkable record of Willie Pep: 212 contests of which he lost only eleven, and seven of those losses came when he was a long way over the hill. Only two men can claim to have beaten the vintage Pep, and both were world champions. Sammy Angott was given a very disputed decision in an overweight match in 1943. Willie was world featherweight champion at the time, having beaten Chalky Wright for the title in 1942. He went into that fight with an unblemished record of 54 fights for 54 wins, and he chalked up another eight wins before the Angott result halted the run. After that, it was five years and another 73 wins before Sandy Saddler stopped him. To recapitulate, 127 fights with one loss before the first decisive claim went against him. Four months after the Saddler debacle, Willie gave the finest displays of his life and one of the most memorable display of pure boxing skill ever seen to regain the title from Saddler.

Willie was a defensive genius and rarely got on the wrong end of a heavy punch. He preferred to win his fights by utilizing the marvellous skills with which he was gifted, but he was no powder-puff puncher and he could, if the occasion demanded, come down off his toes, plant his feet and apply the knockout drop. He was old in boxing terms when he challenged world champion Hogan Kid Bassey very late in his career. His skills had been blunted by then and he was much easier to catch but he was still seldom beaten. It looked as if Willie was going to upset the applecart by outpointing the champion until Bassey broke through his defensive armour in the ninth round. Amidst all the consoling cries of "You were a mile ahead", Pep graciously responded "What does that matter? The Kid had me cold". He retired after that but couldn't make that decision stick and came back in 1965 to run up another ten wins, then hung up his gloves forever when Calvin Woodward outpointed him. Pep was

forty-three and should have been wealthy, but business losses and alimony payments to three ex-wives had diminished his savings. Years after his last fight he is making a fair living with guest appearances and after-dinner speeches, as well as being a class referee. Willie also made a world tour when promoting his autobiography and was received with enthusiasm.

BORN MIDDLETOWN, CONNECTICUT, SEPTEMBER 19 1922
TURNED PROFESSIONAL 1940
WORLD FEATHERWEIGHT CHAMPION 1942–1946 (NYSAC RECOGNITION), 1946–1948 AND 1949–1950
WORLD CHAMPIONSHIP FIGHTS WON 11, LOST 3

His right arm, a trusty weapon in his fighting days, grew weary from the constant signing of autographs. Remarkably, Willie survived an air crash in 1947 when he was en route to London to fight Nel Tarleton. Some of his greatest fights followed but the clash with Tarleton was cancelled.

Among the long list of Pep's victims are the names of Joey Archibald, Allie Stolz, Sal Bartolo, Jackie Wilson, Willie Joyce, Manuel Ortiz, Lulu Constantino, Phil Terranova, Paddy DeMarco, Harold Dade, Ray Famechon, Henry 'Pappy' Gault and Teddy 'Red Top' Davis. Not one of those distinguished pugs could catch up with the fast moving 'Will o' the Wisp', as Willie was termed. His nemesis was Sandy Saddler, who won three out of four of their fights, but the most outstanding of them was the second clash and that went to Pep after a scintillating performance. The last two were rough, foul-filled, bitter encounters that resulted in both men being suspended from boxing in New York State. Willie dislocated his shoulder in their third match and was forced to retire after the eighth round.

As an amateur, he lost only three out of sixty-five outings, one being against the famed Sugar Ray Robinson. Overall, Willie can claim one of the best-ever won-lost boxing records. In a career spanning twenty-six years, he was beaten only eleven times and only Saddler's wins had true merit to them. Sandy was also an all-time great, but he needed the name Willie Pep on his record before he could join that elite club.

Left: Pep, on the right, twice beat Chalky Wright. This 1942 fight was for Chalky's featherweight title.

Below: This is the third of Pep's fights with Sandy Saddler. A dislocated shoulder forced Willie to retire and Sandy went 2–1 up in their four-fight series.

IKE WILLIAMS

BORN BRUNSWICK, GEORGIA, AUGUST 2 1923
TURNED PROFESSIONAL 1940
NBA LIGHTWEIGHT CHAMPION 1945–1947
WORLD LIGHTWEIGHT CHAMPION 1947–1951
WORLD CHAMPIONSHIP FIGHTS WON 9, LOST 1
DIED LOS ANGELES, SEPTEMBER 5 1994

The greatness of Ike Williams, born Isiah Williams in 1923, would have been recognized much sooner in his career had he not been a contemporary of that brilliant heavyweight title-holder Joe Louis. It was, and still is, very much a heavyweight orientated world with a general penchant for viewing those heavy punchers. Ike was in his prime years at the same time that the public demand was on Louis to lead the post-war boxing boom. Heavyweights could hit. Yet this tall, quietly spoken lightweight was a puncher par excellence, to the body as well as to the head. Williams believed in, and practised, the old adage: 'kill the body and the head will die'.

He was an outstanding champion who grew up the hard way, turning professional at sixteen after a short spell with the amateurs. His early management often overmatched him and he was thrown in against Bob Montgomery when he was only eighteen. He got a dreadful beating, but such was the quality of his character he was back in action four weeks later with a first round win, and he eventually thrashed Montgomery in six rounds to get not only revenge but universal recognition as the world lightweight champion.

Williams proved to be an outstanding lightweight and is often accredited with inventing the 'bolo'

punch. This is, of course, a myth – there are no 'new' punches in boxing – but it is a fact that Ike was the first man to show how effective this crippling body shot can be. He used it brilliantly to account for gallant Welshman Ronnie James on a wet evening in Cardiff back in 1946. Ike was defending his version (NBA and NYSAC-recognized) of the world crown. He was hardly at his best because the cold climate got to him, but he was a consummate professional who got on with the job and beat James so decisively that Ronnie was never again a serious contender. One year later Ike had his revenge against Bob Montgomery, but getting down to the lightweight limit was becoming increasingly difficult. He'd put his managerial affairs in the hands of Blinky Palermo who was well connected in the boxing world but who was also a shady character with under-

Right: Ike Williams forces Bob Montgomery into a corner just before the fight was stopped in the sixth round. This was for the lightweight championship of the world, which has been in dispute during the period following the Second World War. Williams avenged a previous defeat by Montgomery and went on to defend his title five times.

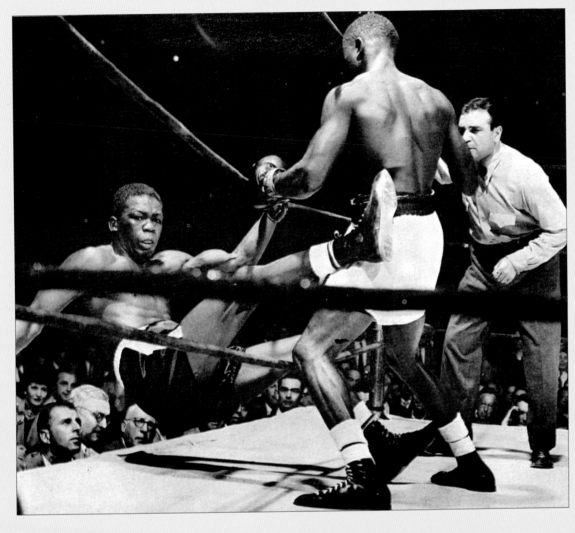

Left: Williams lost his title to Jimmy Carter in 1951. He could no longer make the lightweight limit and was too weak to stand up to Carter's aggression.

world associations. Palermo got his man fights but took most of the money from them. Therefore, when Ike quit boxing in 1955, he had no savings to show for what was a distinguished career.

Williams had designs on Sugar Ray Robinson's welterweight championship. He had successfully defended his own title against outstanding men in Beau Jack, Enrique Bolonas (twice), Jesse Flores and Freddie Dawson. Dawson was the greatest lightweight never to win a title but he could never get past Williams. In four meetings the best he could manage was a draw in 1947. Ike had previously knocked him out, so the 1947 result was quite an achievement. Ike defended his title against Dawson twice and was a points victor both times but was less successful in an incursion into the welterweights as George Costner, who also enjoyed the monikker of 'Sugar', outscored him over ten rounds. Williams forgot all about Ray Robinson and chose to put his title on the line against Jimmy Carter. He suffered agonies in making the weight and fought in such a weakened condition that he took several counts and was stopped

in fourteen rounds. That he lasted so long into the fight speaks volumes for his courage. Williams was never in with a hope but chose to go out on his shield.

The remainder of his career was fought at over ten stone but his great days were over and his record now became spotty. Nevertheless, it took top men like Carmen Basilio and Gil Turner to defeat him, and Ike did get a credible win over Kid Gavilan before bowing out with a fine stoppage over Beau Jack in 1955. On ability and sheer hitting power, he goes into the record books as a very great champion.

In the 1951 investigation into corrupt boxing practices, Ike testified that under manager Blinky Palermo he was often forced to 'carry' his opponent, although his pride would never allow him to deliberately lose a match. Palermo took far more from Ike's earnings than the standard manager's cut and what came Ike's way was too often lost via gambling and handouts to hangers-on, but he never harboured grudges or bitterness and lived contentedly until the age of seventy-one. He died in Los Angeles in 1994.

ROCKY MARCIANO

Rocky Marciano fought forty-nine professional fights as a heavyweight without losing one – a record that many have tried to emulate without success. He was born Rocco Marchegiano, the eldest of six children whose parents were poor Italian immigrants. At school he excelled in several sports, including baseball, but it was boxing that captured his heart. He served in the United States Army at the end of World War Two and, while based in England, made an impression in military boxing competitions. On returning to the United States, he wrote to Madison Square Garden for a trial in the gymnasium and was granted an invitation to perform in front of the famous matchmaker, Al Weill. With no money to his name Marciano hitchhiked from Brockton to New York and was disappointed when Weill and others who watched him were unimpressed. He was considered too small to have any potential as a heavyweight and in addition they reckoned he lacked style.

Marciano returned to his roots, but he continued to box as an amateur while earning a living as a factory worker. He decided to turn professional in 1947 and had a remarkable run of success, winning thirty-five contests in a total of just 146 rounds. This earned him a fight with the much-respected Rex Layne in 1951, and after he won in six rounds, Al Weill started to sing a different tune and took him into his management stable.

Weill matched Marciano against the former world title holder Joe Louis, who gave the youngster something of a boxing lesson but was finally swatted to defeat in the eighth round. The victory over Louis earned Marciano a crack at the world title which belonged to 'Jersey' Joe Walcott. The two met in Philadelphia on September 23 1952 and Walcott knocked the upstart on to the seat of his pants in the

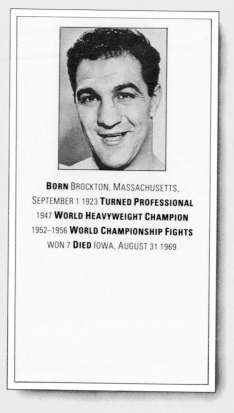

BORN BROCKTON, MASSACHUSETTS, SEPTEMBER 1 1923 **TURNED PROFESSIONAL** 1947 **WORLD HEAVYWEIGHT CHAMPION** 1952–1956 **WORLD CHAMPIONSHIP FIGHTS** WON 7 **DIED** IOWA, AUGUST 31 1969

opening round. Marciano recovered quickly, however, and remorselessly battered the champion into a thirteen-round defeat.

During May the following year Walcott was given a rematch, but his spark had gone and Marciano dispatched him in the opening round. Over the next two and a half years Marciano defended his title five more times. The only man to take him the distance was Ezzard Charles in 1954. His last fight, on September 21 1955, was against Archie Moore who had the satisfaction of putting the champion on the canvas. Marciano once more displayed his phenomenal powers of recovery, and stopped Moore in the ninth round.

After this fight Marciano was determined to spend more time with his family, so he decided, on April 27 1956, to quit boxing while he was at the top. Despite many lucrative offers he steadfastly refused to return to the ring: he was satisfied with the $4 million he had already amassed. Unlike many champions who wasted their wealth, he was financially acute, and had saved and used his money wisely.

Outside the ring Marciano was a mild-mannered, gentle man, but inside he was devastatingly brutal. He was short, just five feet ten and a half inches tall, and he had remarkably small fists for a heavyweight, but what he did have in abundance was physical strength. He could take heavy blows as well as deliver them and what he lacked in technical skills, he made up for with brute force and power. His other great asset was his fitness; he always trained rigorously before a fight and took nothing for granted.

Marciano's final 'fight' was a farcical contest against Muhammad Ali in which the two men acted out a script created by a computer. The machine reckoned that Marciano was the better man and he came out on top with a knockout in the tenth round.

Above: Marciano's most famous punch was unique to him: a swinging right that gave the 'Brockton Blockbuster' two chances to score. If the glove failed to club the side of his opponent's face, the luckless victim would be swatted with forearm and elbow. Given a choice, most boxers would prefer Marciano to land a clean blow with the leather.

Right: Marciano won the heavyweight title from 'Jersey' Joe Walcott in thirteen rounds in Philadelphia on September 23 1952. If most boxers attempted to land a blow from this stance – at right angles to the opponent, and hitting with the left against the grain – it would be too weak to cause problems. With Marciano, it proved to be the first punch in a combination that finished Walcott in the thirteenth.

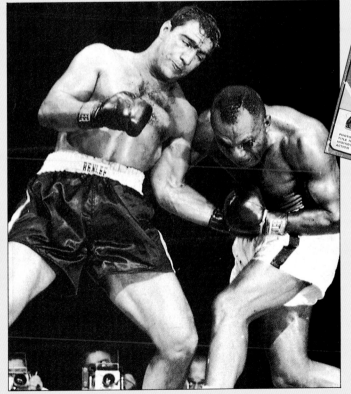

Above: Marciano was beloved by the media and the public. He was a sensible man, who handled his fame with grace. Outside the ring he was kind, gentle, and well-mannered.

SANDY SADDLER

This was no 'Fancy Dan' boxer. Sandy Saddler, born in Boston, Massachusetts, son of West-Indian immigrants, was one of the hardest-punching featherweights of post-war years and he was a rough, tough hombre to boot. He is often remembered for his last fight with arch-rival Willie Pep in which almost every known foul was repeatedly committed. Sandy fell well short of being a dirty fighter but he would respond in kind if he was subjected to rough treatment. Pep found Sandy too tough for him. He didn't like Saddler's power punching and found out that this man could sock as hard as had any featherweight who ever laced on boxing gloves. The one man who may have matched Sandy's reputation was Mexico's Ruben Olivares, but he had 102 contests in a twenty-two year career whereas Saddler scored 103 knockouts over his twelve years of activity. Those figures show the way boxing has changed over the years. Go back to the 1920s, and we find that Johnny Kilbane had 337 fights, but he was no hitter and only twenty-two of his wins came inside the distance. Between November 1944 and September of the following year, Saddler flattened twenty-one of his foes! The most important knockout came in 1948 when he won the featherweight title from the seemingly iron grip of Willie Pep who had breezed through 139 fights with one solitary, and disputed, loss. Pep was never in it when he first met Saddler who put him on the canvas three times before keeping him there for the full count. Sandy was no novice either. He had nearly a hundred fights under his belt before the title shot came his way.

He lost to Pep in the return after what was Willie's greatest performance, then had to wait over a year before he regained it. Pep, trailing on points, quit with a dislocated shoulder. Before this, in late 1949, Sandy picked up the World Junior-Lightweight Championship

BORN BOSTON, MASSACHUSETTS, JUNE 23 1926
TURNED PROFESSIONAL 1944
WORLD JUNIOR LIGHTWEIGHT CHAMPION 1949–1951
WORLD FEATHERWEIGHT CHAMPION 1948–1949 AND 1950–1957

by beating the tough Orlando Zulueta. It was not a highly prestigious title then and it was fought over ten rounds. Saddler defended it twice, knocking out Lauro Salas and Diego Sosa, then relinquished his claim to it. He was still the king of his natural division – the featherweights – and he never lost that title in the ring.

Before regaining his old title, Sandy knocked out Jim Keery on a Jack Solomons' promotion in London. Keery was out of his depth and succumbed to some cruel body punches in the fourth round. On his second visit to Europe in 1954, Ray Famechon went two rounds beyond the limit reached by Keery but he too was stopped.

Saddler was tall and skinny, with tremendous power, but he was surprisingly rugged. He was stopped by Jock Leslie in his second fight but was never beaten inside the distance again. In hindsight it seems very bad management to match a man with the likes of Jock Leslie right at the beginning of a career, but it is noticeable that Saddler was back in winning action less than a week later. After that, it was a steady rise to title contention with the standard of opposition becoming increasingly better. It made little difference. His punches were just as effective against the ten round fighters as they were when he was well down the bill. He lost to the likes of Phil Terranova and Humberto Sierra but Saddler was out of the old school. He treated these losses as learning experiences and got on with his career. Soon he was winning the big matches, but it took him five years to get to the top and that is where he stayed until his last fight in 1956.

Saddler still had prime fighting years ahead of him when he was forced to retire. His eyesight was affected by a traffic accident in 1956. He was passenger in a taxi that was involved in a crash. These were the days prior to those of massive compensation claims and there is no record that Sandy was able to cash in. Despite his

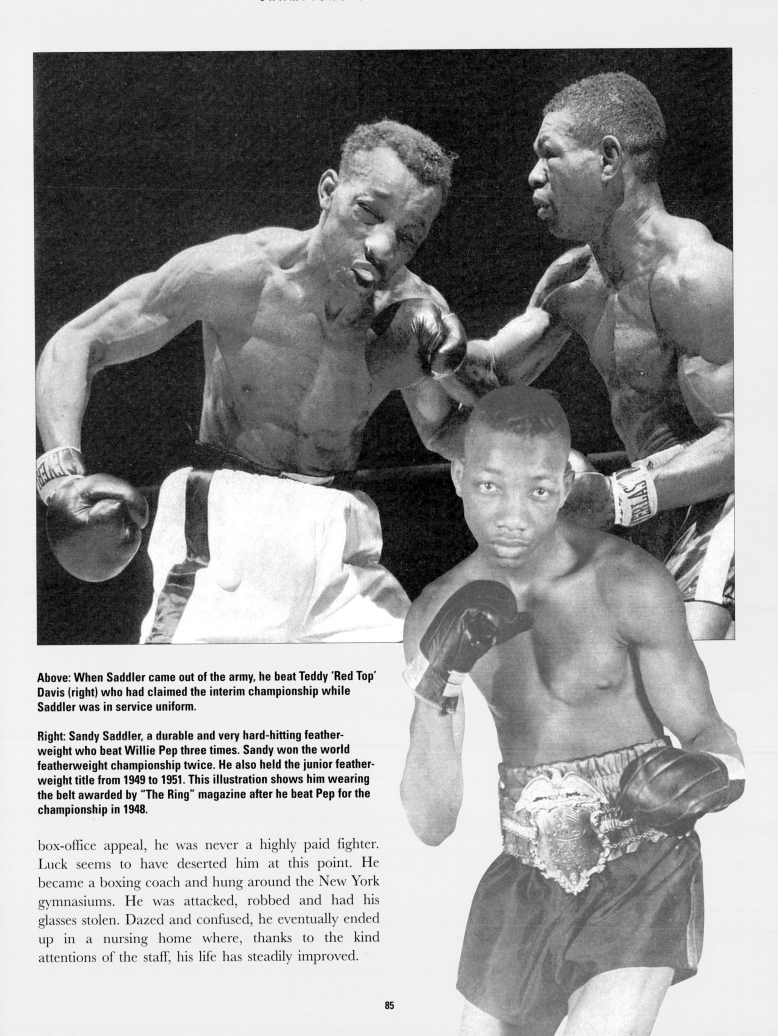

Above: When Saddler came out of the army, he beat Teddy 'Red Top' Davis (right) who had claimed the interim championship while Saddler was in service uniform.

Right: Sandy Saddler, a durable and very hard-hitting feather-weight who beat Willie Pep three times. Sandy won the world featherweight championship twice. He also held the junior feather-weight title from 1949 to 1951. This illustration shows him wearing the belt awarded by "The Ring" magazine after he beat Pep for the championship in 1948.

box-office appeal, he was never a highly paid fighter. Luck seems to have deserted him at this point. He became a boxing coach and hung around the New York gymnasiums. He was attacked, robbed and had his glasses stolen. Dazed and confused, he eventually ended up in a nursing home where, thanks to the kind attentions of the staff, his life has steadily improved.

RANDOLPH TURPIN

One of three famous boxing brothers, Randolph Turpin is regarded by many as having been the most able fighter to have emerged from the English boxing scene since World War Two.

It was while he was serving as a cook in the Royal Navy that Turpin's amateur career began to take off. He won the Amateur Boxing Association (ABA) welterweight title in 1945 when still just seventeen, and the following year he was crowned ABA middleweight champion. Shortly after winning his second ABA title he turned professional and in October 1950 he became British middleweight champion on beating Albert Finch in five rounds. This was sweet news to the Turpin family, as brother Dick had lost the middleweight crown to Finch six months earlier.

Early the following year Turpin took the European middleweight crown in dramatic fashion when he flattened the Dutchman, Luc van Dam, in forty-eight seconds. This remarkable victory put him in line for a world title challenge against the mighty 'Sugar' Ray Robinson. His chance came in July 1951 and he very literally grasped it with both fists, outpointing the American in a memorable bout held at Earls Court in London. A clause in the fight contract stipulated that a return match should be held within sixty-four days, and so it was that Turpin travelled to New York to meet Robinson for a second time two months later. If Robinson had been slap-dash in his preparation for their first clash, he most certainly was not for their second. Turpin appeared to be on the way to a successful defence when, in the tenth round, Robinson surged in and floored the Englishman with a heavy right. Shortly afterwards the referee called a halt and Robinson, complete with a bloody eye, was declared the world middleweight champion once again.

Turpin was never again quite the same boxer after

BORN LEAMINGTON, ENGLAND, JUNE 7 1928
TURNED PROFESSIONAL 1946 **WORLD**
MIDDLEWEIGHT CHAMPION 1951 **WORLD**
CHAMPIONSHIP FIGHTS WON 1, LOST 2
DIED LEAMINGTON, MAY 17 1966

losing his world title, although, at the age of twenty-three, he still had a lot of gusto left in him. In June 1952 he claimed the British and Commonwealth light-heavyweight titles when he humbled Don Cockell, and in the same year he also won the Commonwealth middleweight title from the South African, George Angelo. In June the following year he successfully defended his European middleweight title against a challenge from the Frenchman, Charles Humez. Robinson had temporarily retired at this stage and, outside the United States, Turpin was hailed as the world champion; in America Carl 'Bobo' Olson was hailed as the supremo.

Turpin and Olson duly met to sort out the rivalry on October 21 1953 in New York. Unfortunately the Englishman was dogged by personal problems at the time, and put up a poor showing by his standards, losing the fifteen-round contest on points. More disappointment was to follow. In May 1954 he was knocked cold in sixty-five seconds by the Italian Tiberio Mitri and consequently lost his European middleweight title.

After these two surprise defeats, Turpin's career tailed off. He successfully fought both Alex Buxton and Arthur Howard for the British light-heavyweight title, but after a surprising two-round defeat by Yolande Pompey in 1958, he retired.

Turpin had earned a sizeable fortune in the ring but when he retired he had little of it left. He dabbled in boxing and wrestling promotion for a time but was a tragically unhappy man. Unable to take the burden of financial and domestic pressures he shot himself at home just a few weeks short of his thirty-eighth birthday. That was a sad day for English and world boxing: it lost not only a great personality but one of the most aggressive and hardest-hitting boxers of the post-war era.

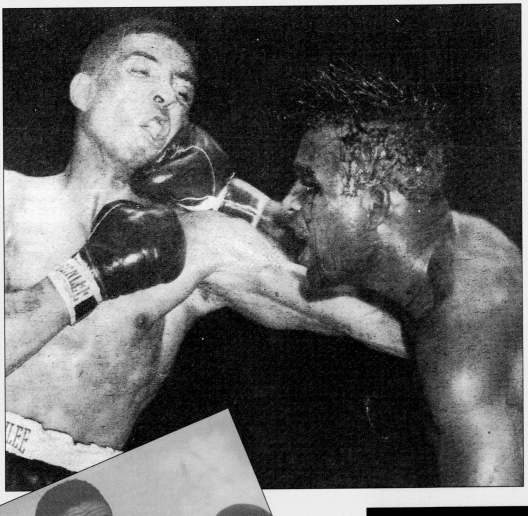

Left and below: The great 'Sugar' Ray Robinson was Turpin's opponent for the two most important fights of his career. In July 1951 Robinson came to London for what was intended to be an easy and lucrative first defence of the middleweight title he had just taken from LaMotta. The odds were twenty-to-one against a British victory, but Robinson was out-of-shape, and Turpin took him on points. On September 12 of the same year (left), a finely-tuned Robinson corrected his mistake by stopping Turpin in ten.

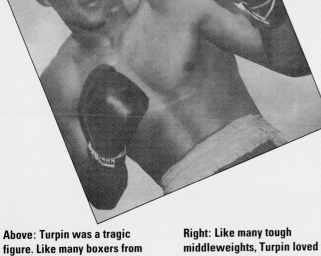

Above: Turpin was a tragic figure. Like many boxers from impoverished backgrounds, he found it hard to cope with the pressures of fame and riches, and this probably contributed to his eventual suicide.

Right: Like many tough middleweights, Turpin loved to take on the big boys. Here he decks Don Cockell to take the British light-heavyweight title on June 10 1952.

INGEMAR JOHANSSON

BORN GOTHENBURG, SWEDEN, OCTOBER 16 1932 **TURNED PROFESSIONAL** 1952 **WORLD HEAVYWEIGHT CHAMPION** 1959–1960 **WORLD CHAMPIONSHIP BOUTS** WON 1, LOST 2

In 1959 Ingemar Johansson became the first European since Primo Carnera to hold the world heavyweight title, and he simultaneously placed Swedish boxing on the map. His amateur career was blighted by a curious decision in the 1952 Olympic Games in Helsinki. He reached the final in the heavyweight division but was disqualified for 'not giving of his best' against the intimidating American, H Edward Sanders; it was not until 1982 that he was finally awarded his silver medal.

After the Olympics Johansson turned professional, and, under the guidance of his canny manager Eddie Ahlquist, made steady progress. He won the European heavyweight title in 1956 by knocking out the Italian, Franco Cavicchi, in thirteen rounds and made an impression on British fight fans a year later when he disposed of Henry Cooper in five rounds. His most impressive win, however, was against the American, Eddie Machen, who was considered to be the number one contender for the world heavyweight title. Johansson dispatched Machen in one round in 1958 on his home turf of Gothenburg and consequently elevated himself into a world championship fight.

Johansson faced the world champion, Floyd Patterson, on June 26 1959 in the rowdy atmosphere of Yankee Stadium, New York. Prior to the fight Johansson and his manager played up the Swede's playboy image and were careful to conceal his devastating right-hand punch from members of the press at the challenger's training sessions. When the day of the fight arrived Patterson was the hot favourite to win, but Johansson unleashed his 'secret weapon' and floored the champion no less than seven times. The contest was stopped in the third round and Europe had its first heavyweight champion for more than twenty-five years.

In the return fight a year later Patterson was fully aware of the potential of Johansson's right hand, and he became the first heavyweight in history to regain his title with an emphatic knockout victory in five rounds. A third match against Patterson in March 1961 proved that the American was the superior boxer – Johansson was counted out in the sixth round of their clash at Miami Beach, Florida.

Right: In an important contest for both fighters, Johansson puts an end to Britain's Henry Cooper in 1957 in the Swedish sunshine. For Johansson, who had won the European heavyweight championship the previous year, it was a valuable stage in rehabilitating his reputation after the 1952 Olympic Games *débâcle*, and the win pushed him further up the ladder towards a world title bout. For Cooper, it meant another few years in the backwoods before a title shot against Ali.

Below: Johansson called his right hand 'The Hammer of Thor', and it was a well-kept secret from American boxers and fight-fans until he unleashed it against Patterson on June 26 1959 in an amazing odds-against victory.

Right and below: Johansson may have looked and behaved like a playboy, but he differed from similar figures like Max Baer in one important respect – he took his fights very seriously. No amount of training and preparation, however, could protect him from Patterson's ire in their June 20 1960 rematch.

On June 17 1962 Johansson regained the European title (which he had been obliged to relinquish when he became world champion) by knocking out England's Dick Richardson in eight rounds. However, he was later stripped of the European title for failing to defend it and in 1963 he decided to embark on another quest for the world title which was at this time held by Sonny Liston. On April 21 he fought England's Brian London in Stockholm in what he reckoned to be a stepping-stone fight for a world championship challenge. He beat London on points but only just: he was floored by a flurry of punches in the last round and would have been counted out had he not been saved by the final bell. Deciding that his match with London was too close for comfort, he acknowledged that it was time to retire.

Johansson's three fights with Patterson had made him wealthy and when he finally hung up his gloves he invested wisely and became a successful business-man. A lover of the good life, he used to frequent clubs and bars even while in training; he also, however, took his fights seriously, even when he pretended that he was doing otherwise. He relied heavily on a right-hand punch, which he kept unobtrusively in reserve until he found an opening in his opponent's defence; most recipients of 'Thor's Hammer' (also known as 'Ingo's Bingo') never knew what hit them and ended up with their backs on the canvas.

HENRY COOPER

Henry Cooper, 'Our 'Enery' to his loyal fans, without doubt remains the most popular British heavyweight since World War Two. He and his identical twin brother, George, who also became a professional boxer, were brought up in Bellingham in south-east London. Henry became a plasterer while at the same time sustaining a successful amateur career as a boxer. In 1952 he won the Amateur Boxing Association (ABA) light-heavyweight title and also represented Great Britain at the Helsinki Olympic Games. He won a second ABA title in 1953 and the following year elected to make a career as a professional.

Cooper experienced mixed fortunes in his early years as a professional. He fought his way up the ladder, but was beaten in nine rounds by Joe Bygraves in 1957 in an attempt to win the Commonwealth heavyweight title. Further defeats by Sweden's Ingemar Johansson and Joe Erskine deprived him of both the European and British crowns.

In 1958 Cooper staged a comeback, and had two impressive victories against Dick Richardson and the American, Zora Folley. These wins marked a turning point in his career and on January 12 1959 he humbled Brian London to gain the British and Empire heavyweight titles. During the next ten years Cooper saw off eight challengers for the British title and thus became the first man in history to win three Lonsdale Belts outright.

Perhaps Cooper's greatest moment came on June 18 1963 when he fought the precocious Cassius Clay (later to become Muhammad Ali) at Wembley Stadium in a non-title fight. In the fourth round he floored Clay with his fabled left hook and the American would almost certainly have been counted out if he had not been saved by the bell. As it was, Clay's trainer, Angelo Dundee, indulged in some time-wasting tactics during the break and when a refreshed Clay succeeded in worsening a cut over the Englishman's left eye during the fifth round the fight was stopped by the referee.

In February 1964 Cooper achieved a points victory over his old adversary Brian London to win the European heavyweight title, and two years later he challenged Muhammad Ali for the world heavyweight crown. At their meeting at Highbury Stadium in London Cooper again put in a courageous effort but the fight had to be stopped in the sixth round because of the blood that was streaming down his face from an open wound above his left eye.

After winning two more European title fights, against Karl Mildenberger in 1968 and Piero Tomasoni in 1969, Cooper was matched against Jimmy Ellis for the WBA world heavyweight crown. However, the British Boxing Board of Control did not recognize the WBA and refused to grant the contest official status, so a disappointed Cooper gave up his British and Empire title in protest.

Overcoming the disappointment of not being allowed to challenge Ellis, Cooper staged a comeback in 1970 and proved his worth by outpointing Jack Bodell to regain the British title. This was followed by another European championship win over Spain's José Urtain. In March 1971, however, Joe Bugner took the British, Commonwealth and European titles from Cooper in a hotly disputed points victory.

Cooper quit boxing after his contest with Bugner and went on to become a highly successful businessman, boxing commentator and star of television commercials. In the ring he was extremely brave and tenacious, which greatly endeared him to a British public starved of boxing success. He is now as much a national institution as a sporting hero.

BORN WESTMINSTER, MAY 3 1934 **TURNED PROFESSIONAL** 1954 **WORLD CHAMPIONSHIP FIGHTS** LOST 1

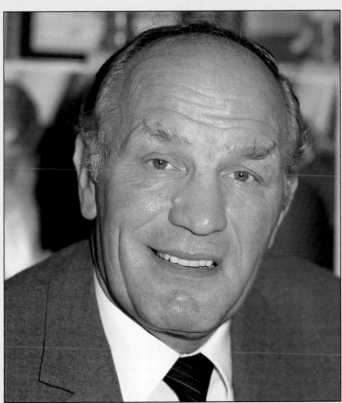

Top: This was Great Britain's most notable challenge for the heavyweight crown in the second half of the twentieth century. The whole nation was emotionally involved in Henry's big shot at the title, but Ali stopped him, again with a cut, in the sixth round on May 23 1966 at the Arsenal soccer ground, Highbury Stadium.

Left: Britain's most popular boxing figure.

Above: Cooper's left eye was badly damaged by young Cassius Clay in the fifth round of their 1963 non-title fight. Henry was a victim of cuts throughout his career: even pictures of his finest victories seldom show him without blood flowing freely on his face. This vulnerability was the principal reason he did not fulfil all of his ambitions.

MUHAMMAD ALI

BORN LOUISVILLE, KENTUCKY, JANUARY 17 1942 **TURNED PROFESSIONAL** 1960 **WORLD HEAVYWEIGHT CHAMPION** 1964–1967, 1974–1978, 1978–1979 **WORLD CHAMPIONSHIP FIGHTS** WON 22, LOST 3

Muhammad Ali once boasted that he was the most famous man in the world, and certainly while he was at his peak his face and voice were immediately recognizable to many millions around the globe. It is beyond doubt that he is the most famous boxer ever, and he has done more to promote the sport than anybody in its history.

He was born Cassius Marcellus Clay, the son of a signwriter whose forebears had been slaves. He started boxing at the age of eleven and had a highly successful amateur career, culminating in a light-heavyweight Golden Gloves award followed by an Olympic gold medal in Rome in 1960.

Returning triumphant from the Olympics he turned professional and after one fight came under the guidance of the trainer Angelo Dundee. He had a flair for creating publicity and one of his gimmicks was to predict the round in which he would defeat opponents. His prophecies proved remarkably accurate and he was consequently labelled 'The Mouth'.

Few pundits gave the twenty-two-year-old Clay much of a chance against the hard-hitting heavyweight world champion Sonny Liston when the two met in Miami in 1964. But Clay ran rings around the champion, who relinquished his title when he refused to come out of his corner at the start of the seventh round. Later in the same year Clay embraced the Black Muslim faith and gave up what he called his 'slave name' to call himself Muhammad Ali.

In his rematch with Liston in 1965, Ali produced a lightning-quick right hand that floored the former champion who was counted out in the first round. Thereafter nobody doubted that the brash young champion could punch as well as he talked. He succeeded in defending the heavyweight title eight more times, including once against England's Henry Cooper, before he was deprived of his crown in 1967 for refusing on religious and moral

Right: A twelve-year-old Cassius Clay has no doubts about where his future will lead him.

Far right: Who could dispute that Ali was king? Not only was he invincible in his prime, but he was also the greatest showman the sport has ever seen. To some, his persistent publicity gimmicks and mouthings became grating: nevertheless, Ali must be credited with pulling boxing out of the doldrums and giving it popular credibility in an increasingly suspicious modern climate.

Left: It is difficult to tell who was more outraged by Liston's pathetic performance in their 1965 rematch – Ali, or the crowd.

Below: Ali at his best against Floyd Patterson.

Above: Ali at his absolute peak – shortly after his Olympic gold medal victory in Rome in 1960, and on his way towards the heavyweight crown only four years later.

grounds to join the United States Army.

Returning to the ring in 1970, Ali lost a title bid against Joe Frazier on points, and then in 1973 he had his jaw broken by Ken Norton. He still claimed he was the 'Greatest', however, and he regained the world title by unexpectedly knocking out George Foreman at a contest held in Zaïre, in 1974.

After successfully defending the title ten more times, including rematches against Frazier and Norton, Ali suffered the third defeat of his career when he lost on points to the relatively unknown Leon Spinks in 1978. Seven months later, though, he became the first man in history to win the heavyweight title three times when he outpointed Spinks in New Orleans.

Ali then retired, but could not resist coming back after a two-year lay-off to take on Larry Holmes for the championship in 1980. Nearly thirty-eight, he was by this time a shadow of his former self and he was stopped for the first time in his career when he retired after ten rounds. One more foolish fight against Trevor Berbick ended in defeat and finished the great champion's career on a sad note.

'Float like a butterfly, sting like a bee' was one of Ali's favourite sayings, and in many respects that is exactly what he did during his early years as a professional. He used to dance round the ring doing his famous Ali Shuffle, pouncing in to strike whenever his opponent lost concentration or became distracted by his outrageous exhibitionism. In later years, when he was heavier, he used different tactics. In his memorable fight against Foreman he had his legion of fans in despair as he absorbed punishment while resting on the ropes. This was all part of his 'rope-a-dope' ploy, and when Foreman had exhausted himself he unleashed his knockout punch.

Suffering from a disease which makes his every movement appear slow and awkward, Ali is now a sorry figure, but still holds the love and respect of fight fans everywhere in the world.

JOE FRAZIER

The seventh son of a large, poor family, Joe Frazier had little to look forward to as a boy. After a spell of working on his father's humble farm he followed the example of his elder brothers and migrated to the metropolis of Philadelphia where he worked as a butcher in an abattoir.

He showed great promise as an amateur boxer and lost only two fights, both to Buster Mathis. It was Mathis who got the better of him in the showdown to decide who would represent the United States as a heavyweight in the 1964 Olympic Games but, as luck would have it, Mathis broke a bone in his hand and it was Frazier who was picked. He did not let his country down and returned from Tokyo with a gold medal, a prize which convinced him that he should turn professional in 1965.

He had an impressive run of success, winning nineteen consecutive fights and beating the likes of Oscar Bonavena and George Chuvalo. In 1968 he was pitted against his old adversary, Mathis, in a fight brokered by the New York Athletic Commission for the world championship. At this time Muhammad Ali had been stripped of his world heavyweight title for not joining the United States Army and rival organizations set up separate competitions to decide who would be 'world champion'. Frazier avenged his two defeats against Mathis by stopping him in eleven rounds. He successfully defended his new title four times, leading to a showdown with the WBA heavyweight champion, Jimmy Ellis, at Madison Square Garden on February 16 1970.

Frazier gave Ellis a ferocious hiding which only lasted four rounds and he was finally acknowledged as the undisputed champion of the world – although faithful followers of Muhammad Ali still claimed that their hero was the best heavyweight around. When

BORN BEAUFORT, SOUTH CAROLINA, JANUARY 12 1944 **TURNED PROFESSIONAL** 1965 **WORLD HEAVYWEIGHT CHAMPION** 1968–1973; (UNDISPUTED, 1970–1973) **WORLD CHAMPIONSHIP FIGHTS** WON 10, LOST 2

Ali returned to boxing the whole world willed him to fight Frazier and in due course a $1 million fight was arranged. In one of the most exciting heavyweight contests in history Frazier outpointed the former champion in New York on March 8 1971.

Two easy fights followed the Ali battle and then, in 1973, Frazier was matched with George Foreman, who was given little chance of victory by the *aficionados* but who pulled off a remarkable victory by stopping the champion in two rounds.

Frazier continued to box after his humiliating defeat by Foreman and gradually won back some of his confidence. He beat the European champion Joe Bugner in a bruising battle before agreeing to a return match against Ali. The second Frazier versus Ali match, on January 28 1974, was another great fight but this time Ali finished victorious on points.

A year later Muhammad Ali was champion of the world once more and Frazier challenged him to a third fight. This was the celebrated 'Thriller in Manila' and it lived up to all expectations. Both men fought courageously but, sapped of energy, Frazier did not come out of his corner for the final round.

Never one to give up easily, Frazier attempted to take his revenge on Foreman in 1976 but lost again in five rounds. He continued to fight until 1981 when he quit after drawing against 'Jumbo' Cummings.

An all-action fighter, Frazier was a hustler who liked to press forward. He was not a particularly big heavyweight but his non-stop approach earned him the nickname 'Smokin' Joe'. When he retired, he tried his luck as a pop singer but it was a career that never really got off the ground. He was more successful at managing his promising son, Marvis, but his hopes were dashed when the young Frazier came unstuck against both Larry Holmes and Mike Tyson.

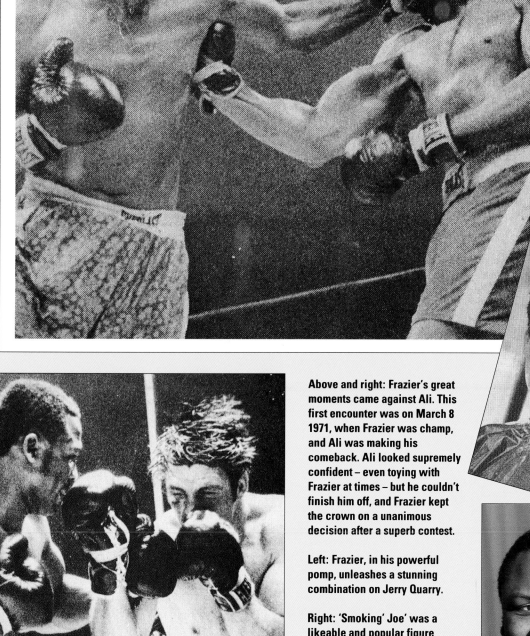

Above and right: Frazier's great moments came against Ali. This first encounter was on March 8 1971, when Frazier was champ, and Ali was making his comeback. Ali looked supremely confident – even toying with Frazier at times – but he couldn't finish him off, and Frazier kept the crown on a unanimous decision after a superb contest.

Left: Frazier, in his powerful pomp, unleashes a stunning combination on Jerry Quarry.

Right: 'Smoking' Joe' was a likeable and popular figure outside the ring. He tried his luck as an entertainer, and stayed involved with boxing by managing his son Marvis.

GEORGE FOREMAN

Born into poverty, George Foreman had a turbulent childhood and might well have taken to a life of crime had he not discovered that organized boxing was a good alternative to a hoodlum's existence on the streets.

He first rose to prominence as an amateur, winning the Olympic heavyweight gold medal in 1968. A year later he turned professional and went through a procession of thirty-seven consecutive victories before confronting the world heavyweight champion Joe Frazier in 1973. At the time Frazier was looking for warm-up fodder for his rematch with Muhammad Ali, and few people reckoned that the hard-hitting Foreman would be serious competition for the champion. It was, indeed, a one-sided contest but very much in Foreman's favour. Frazier was punched all around the ring and went down no less than six times before the referee called a merciful halt in the second round.

The new champion knocked out his first

BORN MARSHALL, TEXAS, JANUARY 22 1948
TURNED PROFESSIONAL 1969 **WORLD HEAVYWEIGHT CHAMPION** 1973–1974; 1994
WORLD CHAMPIONSHIP FIGHTS WON 6, LOST 3

challenger, Joe Roman, in one round and in March 1974 he took on Ken Norton, the man who had gained a fearsome reputation the previous year when he broke Muhammad Ali's jaw. Norton proved no match for Foreman and was dispatched in two rounds.

Foreman's next challenger was the former champion, the great Muhammad Ali. The fight took place in Kinshasa, Zaïre, in 1974, and was dubbed the 'Rumble in the Jungle' by Ali, who, despite all his cockiness, was rated the underdog. For seven rounds Ali allowed Foreman to pummel him as he hung on to the ropes. Then in the eighth, with his man exhausted, Ali caught Foreman on the chin and the champion folded and was counted out.

Shaken by the defeat, Foreman reverted to his former lifestyle and much of the fortune he had earned in the ring was frittered away. In order to try and regain some of his former wealth he came out of retirement, and had convincing victories over Ron

Right: Foreman endeared himself to the American public by unveiling and waving a tiny Stars and Stripes on the winner's podium at the 1968 Olympics. Five years (and thirty-seven victories) later, he was world heavyweight champion, taking the title from Joe Frazier on January 22 1973 on a KO after one minute thirty-five seconds of the second round.

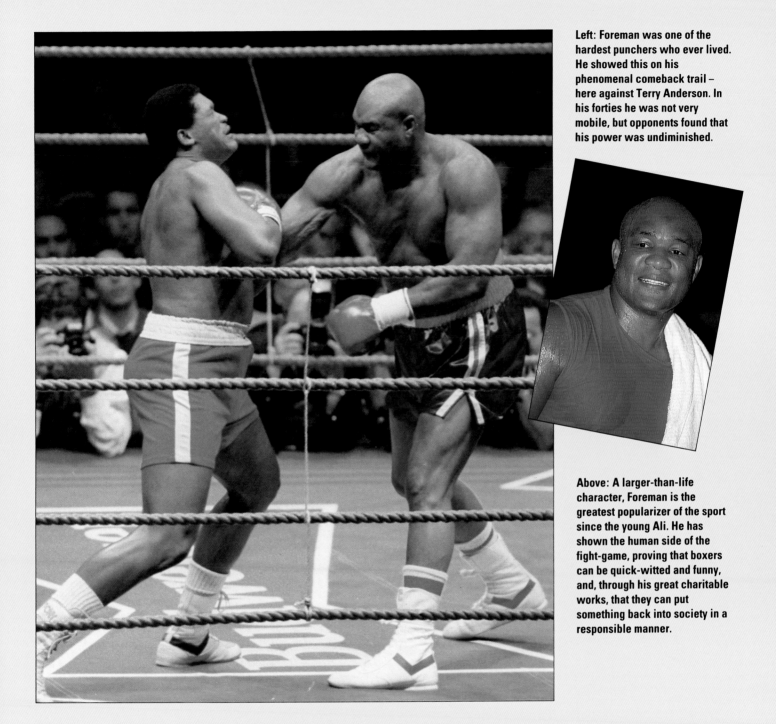

Left: Foreman was one of the hardest punchers who ever lived. He showed this on his phenomenal comeback trail – here against Terry Anderson. In his forties he was not very mobile, but opponents found that his power was undiminished.

Above: A larger-than-life character, Foreman is the greatest popularizer of the sport since the young Ali. He has shown the human side of the fight-game, proving that boxers can be quick-witted and funny, and, through his great charitable works, that they can put something back into society in a responsible manner.

Lyle and Joe Frazier. Then he suffered a shock defeat by Jimmy Young in 1977 and announced to the world that he was giving up boxing to become a preacher.

For ten years, Foreman was out of the reckoning but the call of the ring was too strong and he decided to put on his gloves again and try once more to become world champion. Sceptics were surprised by what they saw. Although the former champion was slow around the ring he still possessed a hugely powerful punch, and his defeat of Gerry Cooney in January 1990 put him in line for a title challenge.

He fought Evander Holyfield in 1991 and Tommy Morrison in 1993 both for versions of the world championship. Although losing, George performed well and when both Holyfield and Morrison were later deposed, he was again poised to challenge for the title. At the age of 46, he became the oldest man ever to win boxing's major prize by knocking out Michael Moorer in the tenth round. He missed a showdown with Mike Tyson when Evander Holyfield got there first, so George defended against Axel Schulz and was stripped of his titles for avoiding his main challengers. In his late forties, he beat Crawford Grimsley; only the obscure WBU recognized it as a title match.

LARRY HOLMES

The life story of Larry Holmes is a classic rags to riches tale. He was one of eleven brothers and sisters, and when he was a youngster he was forced to work as a shoeshine boy to earn much-needed cash for the family. When he was not on the streets seeking customers with tarnished shoes, however, he was in the gym learning to box. He nearly represented the United States at the 1972 Olympic Games but was disqualified in the final of the Olympic Trials for holding Duane Bobick. Not prepared to lose any more time as an amateur, he turned professional in 1973 and launched a career that was to make him a millionaire several times over.

He became recognized as a genuine heavyweight title challenger after twenty-six consecutive victories, twenty of them inside the distance. His chance came in 1978 when he was pitted against the man who had been awarded the WBC version of the heavyweight title, the ageing Ken Norton. They fought a close contest in Las Vegas and Holmes was adjudged the winner on points after fifteen rounds. He successfully defended his title seven times before meeting his boyhood hero Muhammad Ali in 1980. In his youth he had acted as a sparring partner for Ali but by now 'The Greatest' was well past his best and Holmes forced the former champion to retire in the tenth round. 'I love that man and didn't want to see him getting hurt,' Holmes said after his victory.

Perhaps Holmes' most satisfying bout was against the 'Great White Hope', Gerry Cooney, who was convincingly beaten in thirteen rounds but who nevertheless proved to be a courageous challenger. After humbling Marvis Frazier, son of the former heavyweight champion Joe Frazier, in 1983, Holmes relinquished the WBC title and became recognized as heavyweight champion of the newly-formed IBF.

BORN CUTHBERT, GEORGIA, NOVEMBER 3 1949 **TURNED PROFESSIONAL** 1973 **WORLD HEAVYWEIGHT CHAMPION** 1978–1985 **WORLD CHAMPIONSHIP FIGHTS** WON 20, LOST 6

His first defence of the IBF crown was against James 'Bonecrusher' Smith in 1984, and he went on to beat two more challengers before meeting the light-heavyweight Michael Spinks in September 1985. Spinks won the contest on a points verdict that was bitterly disputed by Holmes: it was his first ever professional defeat. In the return match in 1986 Spinks again won on points and Holmes was so unhappy with the result that he announced his retirement from boxing.

Two years later, however, Holmes was offered $2 million to fight Mike Tyson for the undisputed heavyweight championship of the world. It was too much for the thirty-eight-year-old former champion to resist and the two men met at Atlantic City in June 1988. Holmes was painfully and brutally dispatched in four rounds by a man in his prime, who was some seventeen years his junior.

Holmes seldom gets the recognition he deserves as a boxer because he followed in the wake of the irrepressible Muhammad Ali, to whom he is often compared. The two had very different personalities and styles, so any such comparison does not do Holmes justice. He had a formidable left jab and a long reach that he used to good effect. Though not considered to be a knockout specialist, he still stopped thirty-four opponents within the distance.

When in his forties, Holmes announced another comeback and ran up six wins before losing a title challenge to Evander Holyfield in 1992. For two years he went unbeaten. In 1995 he gave the WBC champion Oliver McCall a close fight – despite conceding sixteen years in youth to McCall – and was unbeaten in 1996 before Brian Nielsen edged him out in an IBO title match in Copenhagen. Many at the ringside thought that Larry had won it. He is now hopeful of a match with George Foreman.

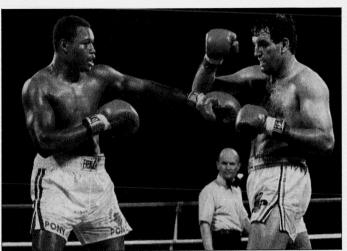

Top, left, and right: Larry Holmes claimed the heavyweight crown between 1978 and 1985, but, despite his terrific record of twenty successful defences (including one against Gerry Cooney, left), he never made his mark with the public, and was not a particularly popular fighter. He retired after losing to Michael Spinks, but was lured back in 1988 to take an unsuccessful crack at Tyson (top).

ROBERTO DURAN

BORN GUARARE, PANAMA, JUNE 16 1951
TURNED PROFESSIONAL 1967 **WORLD
LIGHTWEIGHT CHAMPION** 1972–1978
WORLD WELTERWEIGHT CHAMPION 1980
**WORLD JUNIOR-MIDDLEWEIGHT
CHAMPION** 1983 **WORLD MIDDLEWEIGHT
CHAMPION** 1989 **WORLD CHAMPIONSHIP
FIGHTS** (LIGHTWEIGHT) WON 13
(WELTERWEIGHT) WON 1, LOST 1 (JUNIOR-
MIDDLEWEIGHT) WON 1, LOST 2
(MIDDLEWEIGHT) WON 1, LOST 2 (SUPER-
MIDDLEWEIGHT) LOST 1

Few people ever witness the kind of poverty that Roberto Duran had to endure as a boy. He grew up in his native Panama when he was almost literally required to fight for his survival. With absolutely nothing to lose, he turned professional in 1967 at the age of just sixteen and rapidly built up a reputation that was truly awesome: amazingly, he polished off seven of his first ten victims inside the opening round.

At the beginning of the 1970s, he went to the United States to seek his fortune and was called the 'Hands of Stone', an apt nickname for such a ferocious puncher. On June 26 1972 he was pitted against the WBA world lightweight champion Ken Buchanan in New York. The able Scot was no match for Duran who won when the referee stopped the fight in the thirteenth round.

The new WBA world champion successfully defended his title twelve times against all-comers and only one man, Edwin Viruet, stayed the distance with him. In his final fight as a lightweight, in 1978, against Esteban De Jesus he became un-disputed champion of the world. He then gave up that title in a bid to win the welterweight crown which was then being worn by the great 'Sugar' Ray Leonard.

In a remarkable fight in Montreal in 1980 Duran denied Leonard the space to box in his natural style and dragged the champion into a brawl. It was a tactic that paid handsomely and the Panamanian won an unexpected points decision. In the return match in November the same year Leonard was a wiser man and in the eighth round, in an extraordinary moment, Duran turned his back, saying 'no mas, no mas' ('no more, no more').

Duran's decision to quit against Leonard did little

Right: Pound-for-pound, Duran is placed amongst the great fighters of the twentieth century. Other than the still-mysterious episode against Leonard, in 1980, when he turned his back and refused to fight on, he has the reputation for being a boxer of courage, resilience, determination, and power. He is an old-fashioned street-style fighter, comparable to the likes of LaMotta and Graziano: it is tempting to think that he would have been more at home in the darker boxing world of the 1930s and 1940s, rather than the modern era of Las Vegas, cable TV, and the highly-staged and promoted spectacles in which he has featured so prominently.

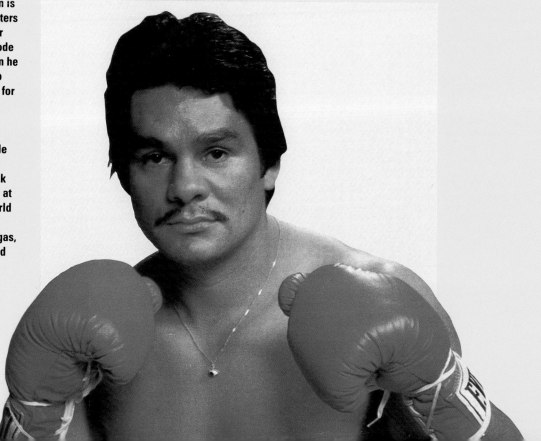

Below: In his thirty-seventh year, Duran still had the power and stamina to beat Iran Barkley and take his middleweight title.

Right: Duran boxed on until his mid-forties: a natural fighter. It is easy to assume that he clung to the ring because boxing was all he knew.

for his reputation and his credibility as a brave and courageous fighter disappeared. He was afraid to return home to Panama and set up home in Miami where he concentrated on training for a shot at the junior-middleweight title. His chance came in 1982, but he lost a points decision to Wilfred Benitez. A year later, however, he stopped Davey Moore in eight rounds to clinch the WBA version of the junior-middleweight title on his thirty-second birthday.

Giving up his new trophy, Duran's next move was to take on Marvin Hagler for the undisputed middleweight crown in November 1983. He lost on points but put on a brave exhibition which went a long way towards restoring his reputation.

Returning to the lower division, Duran challenged the rugged Thomas Hearns on June 15 1984 for the WBC junior-middleweight crown. Hearns proved to be much the stronger man and Duran was knocked out inside two rounds. After this fight Duran quit for a time, but made an extraordinary comeback in February 1989 to take the WBC middleweight title from Iran Barkley in a closely fought contest that resulted in a split decision. This victory sparked off the imagination of promoters who pushed for a final showdown between Duran and Leonard for the super-middleweight title. The fight was an unmitigated flop and Leonard won on points.

Duran is still fighting – often at championship level. He lost a controversial decision in a fight with Hector Camacho in 1996 and, still seeking his 100th victory, gave a good but losing performance against former WBA champion Jorge Castro who is sixteen years his junior.

MARVIN HAGLER

Marvin Hagler, or 'Marvelous Marvin' as the American press dubbed him, was something of a late developer. He turned professional in 1973 and suffered two defeats (later both were avenged) which led observers to believe that he was vulnerable when put under intense pressure. He had been a professional for a full seven years before he had worked his way into a position to challenge for the world middleweight crown. Given the awesome reputation he earned later in his career, it is also surprising that he did not win his first world title bout. It was against the unremarkable Italian, Vino Antuofermo, in Las Vegas in 1979, and although many ringside spectators reckoned that Hagler had done enough to win, the aspiring champion was left disappointed with a draw, and no title. He was soon to put this right.

It was the Englishman Alan Minter who relieved Antuofermo of the world championship in March

BORN NEWARK, NEW JERSEY, MAY 23 1952
TURNED PROFESSIONAL 1973 **WORLD MIDDLEWEIGHT CHAMPION** 1980–1986
WORLD CHAMPIONSHIP FIGHTS WON 13, LOST 1, DREW 1

1980, and in September that year Hagler flew to London for a second attempt at the title. This time he was successful: he severely punished the Englishman, who was so badly lacerated that the referee had to intervene and stop the fight in the third round. Unfortunately Hagler left London with mixed feelings. Although he was ecstatic at having won the championship he was less than happy with the British public's response. Some members of the partisan audience reacted with a vengeance when they saw their man go down. They hurled missiles and racial abuse at the American, who had to have a police escort from the ring to the dressing room. It was a sorry day for British boxing and severely damaged its reputation.

Whether it was in response to the British public's shameful behaviour or not, Hagler was a changed man after his fight with Minter. He disposed of three opponents in rapid order in 1981, and in the spring

Right: These two great ring gladiators, Hagler and Duran, slugged it out in a superbly entertaining and exciting bout in Las Vegas in 1983 for the middleweight crown. At this time the championship was fragmented, with different authorities recognizing different contenders and champions. But as far as the public was concerned, Hagler was the title-holder, and he remained so after defeating Duran on a points verdict.

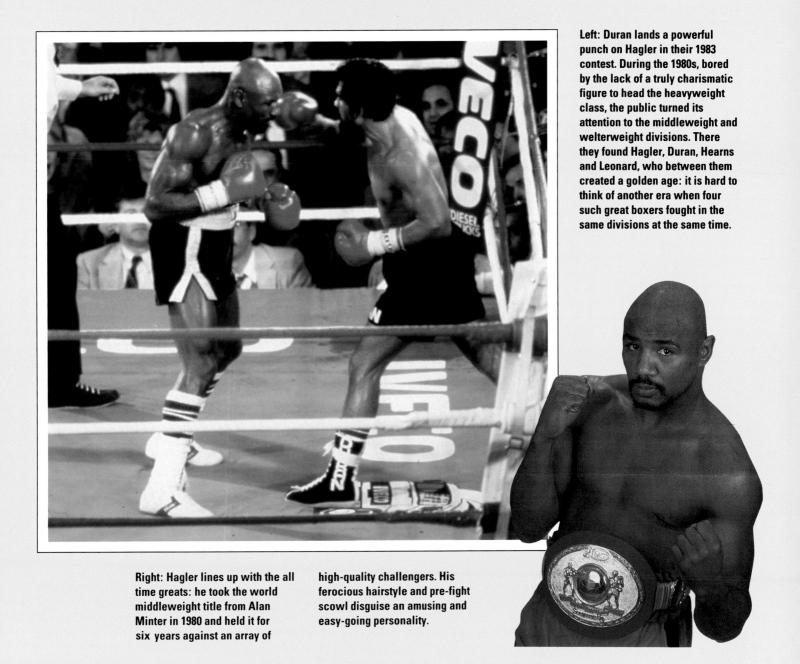

Left: Duran lands a powerful punch on Hagler in their 1983 contest. During the 1980s, bored by the lack of a truly charismatic figure to head the heavyweight class, the public turned its attention to the middleweight and welterweight divisions. There they found Hagler, Duran, Hearns and Leonard, who between them created a golden age: it is hard to think of another era when four such great boxers fought in the same divisions at the same time.

Right: Hagler lines up with the all time greats: he took the world middleweight title from Alan Minter in 1980 and held it for six years against an array of high-quality challengers. His ferocious hairstyle and pre-fight scowl disguise an amusing and easy-going personality.

of 1982 he dispatched William 'Caveman' Lee in just over one minute of the first round. The referee had to save England's Tony Sibson from taking a terrible beating at the start of 1983, and in November the same year Hagler beat the great Panamanian fighter, Roberto Duran, on points in Las Vegas.

One thing Hagler never did was shirk a fight. In 1985, he took on Thomas Hearns in a much-publicized and extremely lucrative fight in Las Vegas. Early on, with a badly cut eye, Hagler was in danger of being stopped, so he went for broke and smashed the 'Hit Man' to the canvas in the third round.

Hagler's next contest was a tough match against the unbeaten John Mugabi, but it all ended for the Ugandan in the eleventh round when he was knocked out. Then in April 1987 came the fight that the world wanted to see: Hagler versus 'Sugar' Ray Leonard in Las Vegas. Huge sums of money had to be placed on the table to draw both men into the ring and it turned out to be the richest fight in boxing history with Hagler getting $17 million and Leonard $11 million. It was a close and thrilling bout with Leonard winning controversially on a split decision. Hagler was sure that he had won, and so deep were his feelings that he never boxed again.

Hagler will always be remembered as a great champion. He was a southpaw with a punishing jab and a devastating right hook and, as if that was not enough, he shaved his head and cultivated a steely stare that put fear into all but the very bravest.

'SUGAR' RAY LEONARD

Leonard was named after the great blues singer Ray Charles by his parents, but he always preferred boxing to a career in music and he began to show off his talents at the tender age of fourteen. He had a meteoric career as an amateur and won the light-welterweight gold medal at the 1976 Olympic Games. After the Montreal games he intended to forego boxing, but was tempted into becoming a professional in order to help pay the family bills and keep them fed.

He started his professional career with twenty-seven consecutive victories and won the WBC world welterweight title at his first attempt in 1979 by stopping Wilfred Benitez in the fifteenth round. He defended the title successfully against Britain's Dave 'Boy' Green in 1980 but then lost the title three months later in an epic battle with Roberto Duran. Recovering well from this setback, he fought Duran again in November 1980 and recaptured the title when, in a notorious and still controversial incident, the Panamanian gave up in the eighth round saying 'no mas, no mas' ('no more, no more').

In June 1981 Leonard stepped up to light-middleweight and took the WBA world title from Ayub Kalule, knocking the Ugandan out in nine

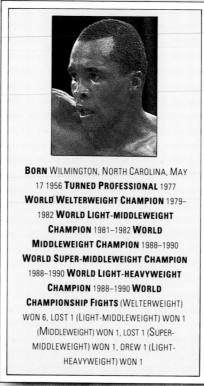

BORN WILMINGTON, NORTH CAROLINA, MAY 17 1956 TURNED PROFESSIONAL 1977 WORLD WELTERWEIGHT CHAMPION 1979–1982 WORLD LIGHT-MIDDLEWEIGHT CHAMPION 1981–1982 WORLD MIDDLEWEIGHT CHAMPION 1988–1990 WORLD SUPER-MIDDLEWEIGHT CHAMPION 1988–1990 WORLD LIGHT-HEAVYWEIGHT CHAMPION 1988–1990 WORLD CHAMPIONSHIP FIGHTS (WELTERWEIGHT) WON 6, LOST 1 (LIGHT-MIDDLEWEIGHT) WON 1 (MIDDLEWEIGHT) WON 1, LOST 1 (SUPER-MIDDLEWEIGHT) WON 1, DREW 1 (LIGHT-HEAVYWEIGHT) WON 1

rounds. Determined to become undisputed world welterweight champion, Leonard then challenged Thomas 'Hit Man' Hearns, the WBA champion. The epic fight lasted for fourteen rounds before the referee called a halt, declaring Leonard the victor.

After humiliating Bruce Finch in three rounds at the beginning of 1982, Leonard was forced to have an eye operation for a detached retina and announced his retirement later in the year. He made a comeback in 1983, but his nine-round win over Kevin Howard was not entirely convincing, and he immediately decided to announce his retirement once more.

Leonard stayed out of the ring for over three years but was tempted back to fight 'Marvelous' Marvin Hagler for the WBC world middleweight title. The fight was held in the car park of Caesar's Palace, Las Vegas, in April 1987 and is reputed to have grossed more than $100 million. With no warm-up fight beforehand, and with only one contest in the previous five years, Leonard boxed his way to a sensational points victory over Hagler.

After winning the richest contest in boxing history Leonard gave up the middleweight crown, but hinted that he might still continue to fight. Sure enough, in November 1988 he fought Donny Lalonde and won in nine rounds. This victory enabled him to claim the WBC light-heavyweight and super-middleweight titles. In 1989, aged thirty-three, he had two more fights: one against Thomas Hearns, with whom he drew, and a second in which he beat, for the second time, the only man who had defeated him, Roberto Duran.

Leonard is regarded as a shrewd tactician and his mastery is beyond doubt but, unwisely, he continued to make comebacks when he was too old for competitive boxing. Terry Norris beat him in 1991 and, six years later, Ray made a vain effort to beat Hector Camacho for the lightly-regarded IBC Middleweight title.

Right: Leonard was an amazing boxer: as much businessman and entrepreneur as fighter, he, above all, was clever enough to benefit from the new era, when boxing contests evolved into a form of world-wide TV spectacle rather than a simple test of strength and skill between two ordinary mortals. At the same time he was a boxer of rare artistry, and an extraordinary mixture of cool intelligence and reckless courage.

Above: 'Sugar' Ray Leonard raises his fist in triumph after a victory over Hagler which confirmed him as probably the richest and most successful boxer of all time. The fight took place on April 6 1987: it was over twelve rounds, in a purpose-built arena in Caesar's Palace parking lot. The decision was split, but went narrowly in Leonard's favour. This was an amazing performance by a man who had been retired for three years and had not even had a warm-up fight to prepare.

Right: Another great money-spinner against Tommy Hearns. What stopped these Leonard/Hearns/Hagler/Duran fights from being perceived as merely cynical paydays (like some of the ludicrous contemporary heavyweight mis-matches) was the quality of the fighting. These men were legitimate pugilists who would have stood their ground in any era, and their battles are an honourable part of boxing's history.

BARRY MCGUIGAN

The son of a singer who had once represented Ireland in the Eurovision Song Contest, McGuigan (who was christened Finbar Patrick) was brought up in Clones, a small town that lies on the border between the Republic of Ireland and Northern Ireland. He showed great promise as a teenager, winning the Commonwealth Games bantamweight gold medal in 1978 at the age of seventeen. However, he disappointed at the 1980 Olympics, where he was eliminated in the second round.

Turning professional as a featherweight a year after the Olympics, under the guidance of Belfast's Barney Eastwood, McGuigan had a setback in his third fight when he was outpointed by Peter Eubanks. Tragedy was to follow in June 1982 when Young Ali, a Nigerian opponent he knocked out in six rounds, died from brain injuries after their fight. But McGuigan was made of stern stuff and he continued to box, relieving Vernon Penprase of the British featherweight title in April 1983. Later in the same year he knocked out Valerio Nati in six rounds to claim the vacant European featherweight title.

After eighteen consecutive wins McGuigan was ready to challenge the veteran holder of the WBA world featherweight title, Eusebio Pedroza, who had remained undefeated since 1978 and had successfully defended his crown nineteen times. Pedroza was reluctant to come to Britain to fight but eventually a price and venue were agreed upon. McGuigan fought Pedroza at the Queen's Park Rangers soccer ground in Shepherd's Bush, London, on June 8 1985 in front of a 25,000 crowd, most of whom were Irish. It turned out to be a remarkable fight with McGuigan flooring the champion in the seventh round and going on to win on points after fifteen rounds.

BORN MONAGHAN, IRELAND, FEBRUARY 28 1961 **TURNED PROFESSIONAL** 1981 **WORLD FEATHERWEIGHT CHAMPION** 1985–1986 **WORLD CHAMPIONSHIP FIGHTS** WON 3, LOST 1

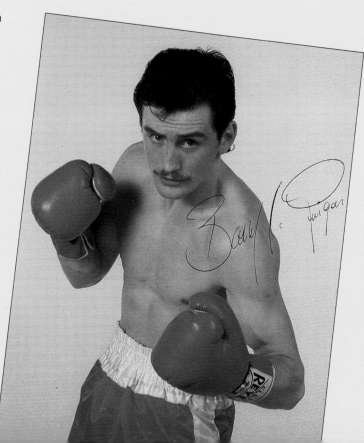

Right: Although a national hero in Ireland, and one of the few boxers from the British Isles to gain international esteem in the last three decades, there is nevertheless a feeling that, with a little luck, McGuigan could have gone further and achieved more. His career was interrupted by injury and by managerial disputes, and a record of four world championship fights does not truly reflect McGuigan's excellence and courage. That having been said, his career record of thirty-two wins from thirty-five outings ranks alongside the very best.

Left and above: Two images from the greatest fight of McGuigan's life – the night he took the title from the great Pedroza. On the left, he has the champion on the run and is moving in to complete a numbing combination. Above, his fans and family chair him in triumph from the ring.

After successfully defending his title twice, McGuigan was lured to Las Vegas where he fought a little-known substitute by the name of Steve Cruz in 1986. After getting the better of the early rounds, the Irishman was troubled by the sweltering heat and succumbed to a points defeat by the young Texan.

For a year or more McGuigan fought a tedious and acrimonious battle with his manager, Eastwood, during which time he was kept out of the ring. He was determined to have another try for the world title, however, and won three comeback contests while under new management. Luck was not with McGuigan, though, and in his fight against Jim McDonnell in 1989 his eye was badly cut and the referee stopped the fight in the fourth round. Deciding that enough was enough, McGuigan retired.

McGuigan developed into an extremely forceful boxer who sapped the strength of his opponents with heavy body blows. He also had a stout heart and a determination that rattled the most experienced of fighters, including Pedroza. His engaging personality has made him a successful television commentator.

The 'Clones Cyclone', as McGuigan was dubbed, hails from a troubled part of Ireland and his popularity was such that both Republicans and Loyalists would flock to see him at Belfast's King's Hall in crowds that were a promoter's dream. He became an Irish hero, and when he beat Pedroza in Shepherd's Bush the folk song 'Danny Boy' was sung by tearful but jubilant Irishmen in pubs and clubs all over the world. His professional record of thirty-two victories, twenty-eight of them inside the distance, out of a total of thirty-five fights shows that in McGuigan all Ireland had a figure of which they could be proud.

AZUMAH NELSON

When he regained the WBC Super-Featherweight championship from Gabe Ruelas in California in 1995, Azumah Nelson underlined his claim to be one of the truly great modern fighters. Long after most boxers are well into their retirement years, the little Ghanaian is boxing better than ever.

The first insight into his abilities came in 1982. As a late substitute, he was considered a sacrificial lamb served up to the legendary Salvador Sanchez in a challenge for the Mexican's WBC featherweight title. Nelson gave the champion a rough ride and Sanchez needed a last round stoppage to save his title. Like all great fighters, Sanchez produced the goods when they were needed but Azumah was having only his fourteenth contest and, although losing, he looked like a future world champion. Seven fights later, by knocking out another great Mexican, Wilfredo Gomez, he became the WBC champion.

Nelson defended the title six times before relinquishing his claim in order to compete at the next highest weight. Nelson is a fighting champion and he chooses his challenges from the top. To date he has notched up 23 world title contests and has but four defeats on a distinguished record.

At super-featherweight level he was matched with tough guy Mario Martinez for the vacant WBC diadem and had to climb off the deck to edge out his opponent on points: only the special fighters can do that. He put the record straight in the return by stopping his man in twelve rounds. He was later to do a similar thing against Jeff Fenech.

There were critics who thought that Fenech had clearly beaten Nelson, that the Australian should have been the new champion and that Nelson was on the slide. Azumah responded by offering Fenech a return in Australia; he answered his critics by taking Fenech

BORN ACCRA, MAY 19 1958 **TURNED PROFESSIONAL** 1979 **WORLD WBC FEATHERWEIGHT CHAMPION** 1984 **WORLD WBC SUPER-FEATHERWEIGHT CHAMPION** 1988 **WORLD WBC SUPER-FEATHERWEIGHT CHAMPION** 1995 **CHAMPIONSHIP FIGHTS** (FEATHERWEIGHT) WON 7 LOST 1 (SUPER-FEATHERWEIGHT) WON 11 DREW 2 LOST 2 (LIGHTWEIGHT) LOST 1

apart and outclassing him with the finisher round eight.

In mid-1990, the Ghanaian set his sights on Pernell Whitaker's IBF and WBC lightweight titles. Whitaker decided to fight off the back foot and ran backwards for the entire twelve rounds. Nelson was unable to catch him and the titles stayed with the champion. That Nelson was slipping was debatable but his subsequent form against Fenech belied such speculation. Never one to make excuses, he did not mention that he had been beset by a bout of malaria and personal problems when he just edged home against Gabe Ruelas in February 1993. The following September he was held to a draw by Jesse James Leija and lost his title to the same man in the return. It began to look as if the ageing African had reached the end of the road.

Nelson was inactive for nineteen months and during this time Leija was deposed by Nelson's old foe, Ruelas. It was a reversal of fortune that put Nelson in line for another fight with Ruelas, with the WBC super-featherweight title at stake.

Factors such as age, inactivity and the loss of form against Leija put Nelson at the wrong end of the betting but what he did that December night is part of boxing's remarkable history. Free of personal problems, fit and finely trained, he turned back the clock, produced a vintage performance and battered the champion to a fifth round defeat. Next, he settled the score with Leija by hammering Jesse to a punishing seven round stoppage.

After seventeen years as a professional, Nelson began to speak of retirement in 1997. He lost his title in March to the former WBA champion, Genaro Hernandez, with Hernandez enjoying huge physical advantages. Nelson has a penchant for doing better the second time around, however, and it could prove unwise to bet against his regaining the title and retiring as the undefeated champion.

OSCAR DE LA HOYA

I f one were to predict which of the current world title holders would be the reigning champion at the turn of the century, Oscar De La Hoya would be that choice. Still only in his early twenties, De La Hoya is a young man and by the time he hangs up his gloves many more titles will adorn his record.

Oscar was the golden boy of the United States at the Barcelona Olympics in 1992. He left the simon-pure ranks with only five losses in 228 contests.

De La Hoya's curriculum vitae after 23 paid wins shows an array of champions and former title holders succumbing to his fistic ability. By beating the formidable John John Molina in 1995, he was named "Fighter of the Year" by the "Ring" magazine. By this time Oscar had already relinquished his IBF lightweight title to pursue the WBC light-welter honours. En route to that diadem, he had taken care of such luminaries as Jorge Paez, Jesse James Leija, John Avila, Rafael Ruelas and the unbeaten

BORN LOS ANGELES, FEBRUARY 4 1973 **TURNED PROFESSIONAL** 1992 **WBO SUPER-FEATHERWEIGHT CHAMPION** 1995 **IBF AND WBO LIGHTWEIGHT CHAMPION** 1995 **WBC LIGHT-WELTERWEIGHT CHAMPION** 1996 **WBO WORLD CHAMPIONSHIP FIGHTS** WON 4

Genaro Hernandez, who was gunned down in six rounds. Hernandez, a former WBA junior lightweight champion, deposed the WBC super-featherweight king, Azumah Nelson, in his next fight. An unstoppable De La Hoya stopped the great Julio Cesar Chavez in *his* next outing and took the WBC light-welterweight crown from the Mexican's head.

He trimmed the iron-jawed Miguel Angel Gonzalez before repeating his win over Chavez, then outpointed Pernell Whitaker and that colourful southpaw Hector Camacho. These were testing fights for the ambitious De La Hoya as was his match with David Kamau in June 1997. Oscar traded punches toe to toe with Kamau and proved that he could go to the trenches if necessary. He got off the deck to beat that classy Ghanian, Ike Quartey, in February 1999 and set himself up for a clash with Felix Trinadad. To his credit, he wants to fight the very cream of the current opposition to clinch his place among the greats.

Right: Golden boy De La Hoya is an unstoppable force in boxing today and is likely to be included on most pound-for-pound lists.

JULIO CESAR CHAVEZ

Many people claim that Julio Chavez is the greatest boxer, pound for pound, of the twentieth century. His record of one defeat in more than ninety professional fights supports that opinion and without doubt he ranks alongside the very best who ever boxed.

He was born and brought up in Mexico where many boys look to boxing as a way of making a living. His three elder brothers all turned professional and Julio Cesar, or 'JC' as he is often called, followed suit in 1980 when he was only seventeen. He had a tough start with twenty-two fights in his first two years, but he won all of them with knockouts.

He won his first world title, the WBC junior-lightweight championship, in September 1984 when he stopped Mario Martinez in the eighth round. He defended the title no less than nine times over

BORN CIUDAD OBREGON, MEXICO, JULY 12 1962 **TURNED PROFESSIONAL** 1980 **WORLD JUNIOR-LIGHTWEIGHT CHAMPION** 1984–1987 **WORLD LIGHTWEIGHT CHAMPION** 1987–1988 **WORLD JUNIOR-WELTERWEIGHT CHAMPION** 1989–1994 **WORLD CHAMPIONSHIP FIGHTS** (JUNIOR-LIGHTWEIGHT) WON 10 (LIGHTWEIGHT) WON 3 (JUNIOR-WELTERWEIGHT) WON 14 LOST 1 (WELTERWEIGHT) DREW 1

the next three years, winning all but four of the contests inside the distance. Among his victims were Roger Mayweather who went out in two rounds, and Rocky Lockridge who managed to survive for the full twelve rounds but lost on points.

Late in 1987 Chavez gave up his junior-lightweight crown and stepped up to lightweight, relieving Edwin Rosario of the WBA world title in November. Almost a year later he was able to add the WBC lightweight prize to his trophy cabinet when he got the better of José Luis Ramirez in Las Vegas.

In the spring of 1989 Chavez moved further up the weight ladder to fight his old adversary Roger Mayweather for the WBC junior-welterweight world championship. The referee had to stop the fight in the tenth round, declaring Chavez the winner. After picking off two contenders for his

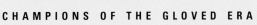

Below: Chavez is so good, that if he is run close in a bout it makes the headlines. Probably his hardest fight was against Meldrick Taylor in 1989: JC, behind on points in the last round, saved the day by a crushing attack which finished the bout with only two seconds left on the clock.

Right: Chavez prepares to despatch Ramirez. Although it is impossible, and invidious, to make comparisons between weights and decades, if the title Fighter of the Century was on offer, Chavez would be one of the most serious contenders.

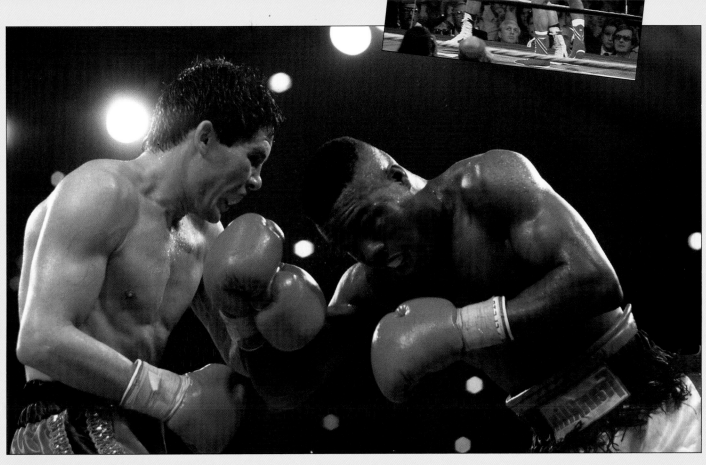

new title late in 1989, a contest was arranged between Chavez and Meldrick Taylor who was in possession of the IBF junior-welterweight crown. In a bitterly-fought brawl in Las Vegas Chavez looked in danger of losing, but in the final round he produced a whirlwind of punches and the referee stopped the fight. It was a close call for Chavez: there were just two seconds to go on the clock!

Taylor had to wait five years for a return but his best days were then behind him and he was comprehensively beaten in eight rounds. Chavez had ambitions at welterweight level and forced WBC champion Pernell Whittaker to a draw in 1994 after successfully defending his junior welterweight title against Terrence Ali.

Chavez's long winning streak was broken in his 90th fight when slick boxing Frankie Randall floored and outpointed him. Randall was boxing well in the return match when a cut, caused by a head clash, made it impossible for the Mexican to continue. Chavez was awarded a 'technical' points win and thereby regained his title.

If critics considered Chavez to be on the slide, his impressive win over former champion Tony Lopez silenced them.

Oscar De La Hoya, a young, unbeaten and potentially great boxer, was the man who dented the legend of Chavez's invincibility. A clash of heads in the first round cut Julio badly and the injuries had so deteriorated by the fourth round that the referee called a halt. Chavez fought with much of his old venom in the return but injuries again forced him to haul down his flag.

MIKE TYSON

Mike Tyson was born and brought up in one of the grimmer ghettos of New York City, and as a young teenager he discovered that the easiest way to get money was to mug people. He learned to box in a reform school for delinquents where he was spotted by Cus D'Amato, who had managed the former world heavyweight champion, Floyd Patterson. D'Amato recognized the reckless fourteen-year-old's potential and became his legal guardian, friend, father-figure and mentor.

Under the expert tutelage of D'Amato, Tyson flourished: he had mixed success as an amateur, but won the Golden Gloves heavyweight championship in 1984. He turned professional in 1985 and rapidly earned a formidable reputation as a knockout specialist, disposing of fifteen opponents in a total of just twenty-two rounds. In his second year as a professional he had thirteen straight wins before being pitted against the WBC world heavyweight champion, Trevor Berbick. Tyson despatched Berbick in two rounds and, at twenty years and 145 days, he became the youngest man ever to claim a world heavyweight title. In March 1987 he took on the mighty James 'Bonecrusher' Smith for the WBA heavyweight crown. Smith retained some credibility by going the distance, but he lost his title on points.

Over the next two to three years Tyson put away ·eight challengers, including the former champion Larry Holmes in four rounds, and Frank Bruno in five in February 1989. One of his most remarkable fights was against the unbeaten Michael Spinks who lasted a paltry ninety-one seconds in a contest held in Atlantic City in 1988. A quicker victory was to follow, however: on July 21 1989 he knocked out the IBF champion Carl Williams in just eighty-three seconds, which confirmed his status as undisputed heavyweight champion of the world.

BORN BROOKLYN, NEW YORK, JUNE 30 1966
TURNED PROFESSIONAL 1985 **WORLD HEAVYWEIGHT CHAMPION** 1986–1990
WORLD CHAMPIONSHIP FIGHTS WON 11, LOST 2

Many thought Tyson to be unbeatable, but Frank Bruno had shown that the champion could at least be hurt; the Englishman had temporarily stunned Tyson with a clip to the head during the first round of their 1989 contest. Then in 1990 occurred one of the greatest upsets in boxing history. Tyson faced James 'Buster' Douglas in Tokyo and virtually nobody gave the challenger a chance. In the eighth round it all seemed to be over when Douglas went down for what turned out to be a 'long count', but he got up and continued to box. By this time Tyson was tiring and Douglas finished the fight in the tenth round. Some controversy raged over the long count, mainly whipped up by Tyson's new handler, Don King, in an attempt to get the verdict quashed, but Douglas was heralded as the new champion.

Douglas' reign as champion was short-lived, and he lost to Evander Holyfield later in the year. Tyson immediately sought a showdown with Holyfield, but their proposed fight in November 1991 had to be postponed due to an injury sustained by 'Iron Mike'.

Tyson is an all-action, aggressive fighter with a solid punch in each hand. Until he was stopped by James 'Buster' Douglas, his aura of invincibility was such that most opponents were beaten before they got into the ring.

A much-publicized divorce and a rape conviction sullied his public image and Mike served a jail term during which boxing declined. He scored a couple of quick wins upon release and regained the WBC title from Frank Bruno. He was not ready for such a demanding match as that with Evander Holyfield who stopped him after a great fight. Mike got a return, but his volatile temper surfaced when a butt cut him above the eye. He was disqualified for biting Holyfield's ear. His halcyon days are gone, but Mike's appearance in a boxing ring will still generate millions of dollars.

Above: Leaving aside events away from the ring, Tyson must be viewed as a truly exceptional champion – a colossus who dominated his age, albeit during a truncated reign. If his power and aggression could have been properly harnessed and controlled, he might well have been the greatest ever.

Right: There was little artistry in Tyson's ring technique, but his brute power and sheer savagery were enough to see off all-comers. Of past greats, the most obvious comparison is with Marciano, and a fight between the two would have been spectacular indeed.

RIDDICK BOWE

By impressively deposing Evander Holyfield in a classic, all-action encounter, Riddick Bowe emerged as a formidable heavy-weight champion. Some critics had expressed prior doubts as to his 'heart' and durability – citing his struggle to outpoint former WBA champion, Tony Tubbs – but the way in which he beat Holyfield soon made them change their tune.

Bowe went into the fight with thirty-one victories and an unbeaten professional record that included the scalps of Everett Martin, Bert Cooper and former WBC champion, Pinklon Thomas. His first defence emphasised his power when Michael Dokes failed to last one round. Yet Dokes was a former WBA champion!

The WBC tried to enforce an agreement that Bowe should defend against Lennox Lewis, rather than against Dokes, so Riddick promptly relinquished the WBC title. After dropping the WBC belt in a

BORN BROOKLYN, NEW YORK, AUGUST 10 1967 **TURNED PROFESSIONAL** 1989 **WBA AND IBF CHAMPION** 1992–93 **WBO HEAVYWEIGHT CHAMPION** 1995 **WORLD CHAMPIONSHIP FIGHTS** WON 5, LOST 2

rubbish bin, he invited Lennox to remove it if he so desired. Lewis is the last man to have beaten Bowe. That was at the 1988 Olympic finals when family misfortunes were, perhaps, playing on Riddick's mind and impeding his concentration.

Bowe put on weight and eventually lost his title to Holyfield in their second meeting in 1993. Once again it was a magnificent battle and Bowe was great in defeat.

Putting that loss behind him, he carried on winning. He beat Herbie Hide in six rounds for the WBO title in March 1995 then went on to outclass the giant Cuban Jorge Gonzalez. He then stopped his old foe, the formidable Evander Holyfield, in a battle of a rubber match. The Polish hard-man Andrew Golota had two brutal encounters with Bowe and lost them both on fouls after each man had given out and received severe punishment.

Right: Bowe in unstoppable form against Bruce Seddon in Atlantic City. The New Yorker knocked the 'Atlantic City Express', once ranked world number eleven by the WBA, to the canvas twice – the second time clinching the bout.

LENNOX LEWIS

Lennox Lewis turned professional after winning the 1988 Olympic heavyweight championship. He notched up eleven quick wins, then he outpointed former WBA cruiserweight champion Ossie Ocasio. From then on he was a main event fighter.

Just sixteen months into his pro career, he stopped Jean Chanet for the European title and then added the British crown by stopping Gary Mason. In his American debut, he impressively knocked out former WBA kingpin Mike Weaver. Tyrell Biggs, still a class fighter, was then knocked out in three rounds.

After annexing the Commonwealth championship, he annihilated the feared Donovan 'Razor' Ruddock in two of the most explosive rounds seen in a British ring. The WBC then recognized Lewis as champion after Riddick Bowe refused to fight him. To cement his claim as title-holder, Lewis outscored top contender Tony Tucker in Las Vegas, then after a slow start, stopped Frank Bruno in Cardiff.

A brief lapse in concentration cost Lennox his title in 1994. He was beaten to the punch and was surprisingly stopped by Oliver McCall. McCall lost his crown to Bruno and the heavyweight field was again wide open. Lewis came back in style to stop Tommy Morrison and Lionel

BORN LONDON, SEPTEMBER 2 1965
TURNED PROFESSIONAL JUNE 1989
BRITISH, COMMONWEALTH &
EUROPEAN HEAVYWEIGHT CHAMPION
AWARDED **WBC WORLD**
HEAVYWEIGHT CHAMPIONSHIP
REGAINED WBC TITLE IN 1997
WORLD HEAVYWEIGHT CHAMPION
NOVEMBER 1999 RECOGNISED BY ALL RULING
BODIES AFTER DEFEATING EVANDER HOLYFIELD

Butler, then showed stamina and grit when outpointing Ray Mercer over ten hard-fought rounds in New York.

In 1997 Lewis beat his old foe Oliver McCall in five rather bizarre rounds for the vacant WBC title. McCall had a mental illness and was in tears before quitting. Lewis had erased the only blot on his record. His first challenger was Henry Akinwande who was disqualified for holding. This preceded the best performance of Lewis's career. In a chilling display of power punching, he blasted out danger-man Andrew Golota in 95 seconds and paved the way for a unification fight against Evander Holyfield, who was the WBA and IBF champion. Lewis kept busy during the protracted negotiations with wins over Shannon Briggs and Zeljko Mavrovic. It was March 1999 before he and Holyfield faced each other in New York. The decision was a draw, but most critics had scored it for Lewis. A return match was made eight months later. Lewis survived a mid-fight surge by Holyfield and finished strongly to win.

So the century closed with a British-born heavyweight champion at the helm. It had been a long wait since 1899 when Cornish-born Bob Fitzsimmons ruled the heavyweight world.

Right: Lewis floors the Canadian Donovan 'Razor' Ruddock for the second and final time in the second round of their World Boxing Council final eliminator at London's Earls Court Arena in December 1992. In a study of controlled aggression, Lewis made easy work of the man who had gone nineteen rounds with Mike Tyson. When Riddick Bowe refused to defend against Lewis, the WBC withdrew recognition of him as champion and awarded Lennox Lewis the title thanks to his impressive victory over Ruddock.

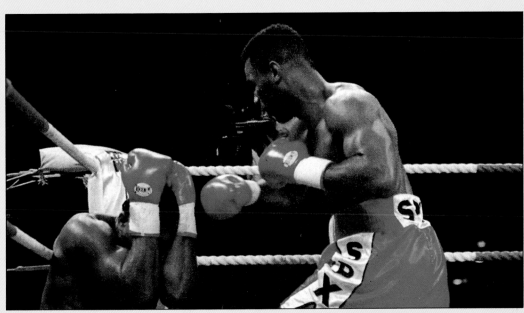

NIGEL BENN

The sobriquet "Dark Destroyer" was not bestowed lightly on Nigel Benn. He has been one of the best value for money attractions fighting at the 12 stone limit for many years.

Benn has consistently stepped in against men that other champions have avoided, and his self-confidence has helped him to bring off some spectacular victories. Only three men have beaten him in a 45 fight career – namely, Michael Watson, Chris Eubank and Sugar Boy Malinga – and all of those had to be at their best to add Benn's scalp to their scoreboards.

Benn picked up the vacant Commonwealth Middleweight in 1988 and defended it thrice with ease; nobody since Reggie Miller ten fights previously having taken him past the second round. It was Michael Watson who brought the success story to a halt in a classic fight at Finsbury Park in 1989.

That loss was a watershed in Nigel's career. Many a fighter would have been discouraged at having his limitations so cruelly exposed but Benn is made of stern stuff. He took a five-month break and shifted his base to America. Solid gym work proved so beneficial that he scored his first points win in Atlantic City against Jorge Amparo then polished off Jose Quinores in one round.

1990 was the year that Nigel emerged as a world-beater. He took Doug DeWitt's WBO middleweight title with a display of punching that finished the American as a top fighter; one of the best performances by a British middleweight in the USA followed when he sensationally crushed dangerous Iran Barkley in one round.

Returning to England, Benn lost his title to Chris Eubank in an epic scrap at Birmingham. Fortunes fluctuated until superb physical condition enabled Eubank to outslug and to stop Benn. Nigel offered

BORN ILFORD, JANUARY 22 1964 **TURNED PROFESSIONAL** JUNE 1987 **WBO MIDDLEWEIGHT CHAMPION** 1990 **WBC SUPER-MIDDLEWEIGHT CHAMPION** 1992 **CHAMPIONSHIP FIGHTS** (WBO MIDDLEWEIGHT) WON 2, LOST 1 (WBO SUPER-MIDDLEWEIGHT) WON 8, LOST 3, DRAWN 2

no excuses but asked for a return. He had to wait three years. Eubank was then WBO Champion and seemed very fortunate to get a draw. Nigel held the WBC title at the time and was trying to unify the two versions of the championship.

He'd won the WBC crown against an Italian in Italy! Mauro Galvano was forced to quit after a three round battering. Six defences followed, three of which went the distance, causing a rumour that Benn had lost his punch.

In February 1995 Benn responded to that theory when he faced the much-feared Gerald McClellan – a power puncher with 20 first round wins in 33 fights. McClellen was a clear favourite to win and win quickly. It looked as if he would do just that when he put Nigel through the ropes in the first minute. Benn got up and hung on. By the end of the round, he was fighting back, and in the second he fought so hard that McClellan was shaken. They went at it hammers and tongs for ten rounds before the American dropped to one knee and took the full count. Benn's triumph in this savage battle was muted by McClellan's subsequent admission to hospital with a brain injury. This took the gilt off Nigel's magnificent performance, but he is a professional and this is his living.

This hard-won victory took something out of Benn. He stopped both Vincenzo Nardiello and Danny Ray Perez but appeared to lack motivation. When Sugarboy Malinga surprisingly outpointed him in March 1996, Benn's title was lost and in defeat he was a shadow of his former self. He announced his retirement but later decided against it and went on to challenge – twice – the WBO champion, Steve Collins. Benn failed to last the distance on both occasions. The well was dry and Nigel announced his retirement at the end of 1996.

ROY JONES

Roy Jones emerged as one of the superstars of the 90s when he took the IBF Super Middleweight Championship from an outstanding title holder in James Toney. There were those who favoured Jones to win but the odds were short whoever you chose. It was a classic pairing, full of imponderables, between two men who went into the Las Vegas ring with unblemished professional records. It looked like being a close, hard-fought battle with Toney a slight favourite in the opinion of the cognoscenti. In the event, Jones won clearly and the manner of his victory sent the press reporters searching for superlatives to describe the skills of the new champion.

Jones had turned twenty before he boxed for pay. He entered the pro ranks with a wealth of amateur experience behind him. He was a silver medal winner in the 1988 Olympics with the Val Barker trophy awarded to him as a bonus.

He'd been a professional for four years before he was taken to a points win. Jorge Castro lasted the 10 round course in Jones's home town of Pensacola and by then Jones seemed a cert bet for world title honours.

BORN PENSACOLA, FLORIDA, JANUARY 16 1969 **TURNED PROFESSIONAL** 1989 **IBF MIDDLEWEIGHT CHAMPION** 1993 **IBF SUPER-MIDDLEWEIGHT CHAMPION** 1994 AWARDED WBC (INTERIM) LIGHT-HEAVYWEIGHT CHAMPIONSHIP 1996 **WORLD CHAMPIONSHIP FIGHTS** (MIDDLEWEIGHT) WON 2 (SUPER-MIDDLEWEIGHT) WON 6 (LIGHT-HEAVYWEIGHT) LOST 1, WON 1

He'd knocked out Ricky Stockhouse, Reggie Miller and – ominously – former world welterweight champion Jorge Vaca. Vaca lasted less than a round, as had Art Servano and Glenn Wolfe.

Jones got his first world title shot at the middleweight limit in 1993 and clearly outpointed Bernard Hopkins for the vacant crown. Hopkins was made to look very ordinary and Jones extended himself only enough to clinch the decision. He'd shown the same casual approach before. "Professional boxing is all business and I do only what I need to. Only if the money is adequate will I extend myself", was his response.

At the Super-Middleweight limit, Jones showed the killer streak. After beating Toney he stopped Antoine Byrd, Vinnie Pazienza, Tony Thornton, Merqui Sosa, Eric Lucas and Bryant Brannon before outscoring his friend Mike McCullum for the Light-Heavyweight title. In his first defence, he blotted his record by hitting Montell Griffin when the challenger was down, thus earning a disqualification from the referee. Jones won the return in one round and has never come close to being beaten since then.

Right: Roy Jones moment of triumph, as he salutes his new IBF Super Middleweight World Championship victory over James Toney on November 18 1994. Jones's superior ringcraft and lightening quick hands and feet saw him home against an opponent who was sluggish on the night.

BRITISH STARS

Left: Terry Downes was born in London on May 9 1936. After a successful amateur and army boxing career he turned professional in 1957. He became British middleweight champion on defeating Phil Edwards on September 30 1958, and world middleweight champion on beating Paul Pender on July 11 1961. He fought forty-three professional bouts, winning thirty-four; twenty-seven of his victories were knockouts.

TERRY DOWNES
MIDDLEWEIGHT

Downes was born in 1936 in London's Paddington district. After military service – some of which was spent in the United States in the Marine Corps – he turned professional, and took the British middleweight title from Phil Edwards in his twentieth bout. After some domestic ups and downs, he earned a world title eliminator against the highly experienced Joey Giardello: to everyone's, except Downes', surprise, he gave Giardello a boxing lesson, tempering, for once, his rushing windmill style to mix in a few artistic jabs.

On January 14 1961, Downes got his shot at the new champion, Paul Pender, who had taken the crown from Sugar Ray Robinson the previous year. Probably over-awed, he wasted the opportunity by attempting to go forward too relentlessly, and received such a badly gashed nose that the fight was stopped in the seventh round. Sensing an easy and lucrative rematch, Pender agreed to come to London for the return.

On July 11 1961 Downes achieved his dream of a world title by stopping Pender after nine rounds. The fight ended oddly and suddenly: Pender was ahead on points, and did well in the ninth round, but he stayed on his stool for the tenth. The air of controversy robbed Downes of some of the glory he deserved.

Downes lost a return with Pender in Boston on April 7 1962 by a unanimous decision. He boxed on, but, other than a rather sad win against his boyhood hero Sugar Ray Robinson, had only one more fight of international significance, in 1964. This was against Willie Pastrano, who had become the world light-heavyweight champion in June 1963. In their encounter, which was for the world light-heavyweight title Downes ran him desperately close, but lost on a stoppage.

Downes was much loved both in the ring and after his retirement. A natural character, with no airs or graces, he stayed in the boxing world and used some of the great wealth he had shrewdly accumulated for the good of the sport and for many charities.

JOHN CONTEH
LIGHT-HEAVYWEIGHT

Conteh's story is similar to Barry McGuigan's: he achieved a lot by ordinary standards; won a world title, and became a hero to his people – yet somehow he never fulfilled his potential, and a question is left hanging about what might have been.

His career was launched in 1970 when he won a Commonwealth Games middleweight gold medal aged nineteen. He beat the fine German, Rudiger Schmidtke, in 1973 to take the European light-heavyweight crown, and a match was arranged with the other great British favourite of the time, Chris Finnegan, to settle the British and Commonwealth titles. Conteh won the first match and a controversial return, proving himself the best in Britain. The manner of his victories, and his all-round win-at-all-costs approach, ensured that, although he was undoubtedly the most admired and respected boxer of his generation, some elements of the 'sporting' British public (who tend to favour a good loser over an out-and-out winner) never took him to their hearts. An exception was the fans in his hometown of Liverpool, who adored him.

Conteh had earned a shot at the world title, and was lined up to fight the Argentinian, Jorge Ahu-

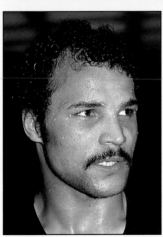

Above: John Conteh. Top: Conteh in action against Parlov in Belgrade.

mada, for the light-heavyweight title vacated by Bob Foster. The battle took place at Wembley Pool, London, on October 1 1974, and Conteh was not about to lose. He contested every second of a brutal fifteen rounds, emerging the points victor.

Conteh defended his title three times in the next three years, against Lonnie Bennett, Yaqui Lopez, and Len Hutchins, but neither the quality of the opposition, nor the frequency of his outings impressed the boxing authorities, who stripped him of the title. In truth, things had gone wrong for Conteh at this stage: he got entangled in disputes with his managers, and he was sidetracked by the lifestyle his fame and filmstar looks had brought him. He had chances to come back, and was the victim of an awful decision against Parlov in Belgrade, but his career was ended when his licence was revoked on medical grounds.

JOE BUGNER
HEAVYWEIGHT

Bugner was born in Hungary in 1950, and was raised in Great Britain, where he took up citizenship. His personality, like his career, was an enigma from start to finish. Here was a boxer who had been given everything, and whose obvious potential should have made him a natural hero to a nation that could never remember having had a world heavyweight champion: yet he never gelled with the British fight fans, and in retrospect it was this lack of support and sympathy that contributed as much as anything to Bugner's alienation and his failure to fulfil his dreams.

The real watershed in his career occurred not in the world title challenges that came later, but in a parochial match for the British championship at Wembley Pool on March 16 1971 in front of an audience of 10,000 baying enthusiasts. The opponent was Henry Cooper, and all but a handful of the crowd had paid good money to see their hero whip the twenty-one-year-old upstart: but Bugner beat Cooper on a highly controversial points decision, and if he had knocked out the Queen of England it would have left him more popular with the fans.

Bugner went on to achieve more in the ring than any other British

Left and above: Joe Bugner, the man the British fans refused to love. He had a tremendous physique, and all the attributes and requirements of a great heavyweight, but never managed to put it all together to the satisfaction of the crowds.

heavyweight for fifty years, yet he would always be known as the man who beat Cooper. He fought Ali twice: the first, a tremendous non-title twelve round match in Las Vegas, and the second, a disappointing, lacklustre fifteen rounder for Ali's championship. This was contested in the enervating Kuala Lumpur heat and Ali was back to his old form. Three months later he beat Joe Frazier in

that memorable fight in Manila.

Bugner had enjoyed his finest moment against Frazier soon after his first loss to Ali. The Britisher climbed off the floor to give Frazier a very close fight but he was never again as impressive and he took up Australian citizenship. He ran up some good wins against rated Americans when domiciled 'down under'.

After a long absence, he made a comeback against Frank Bruno in England but was too far past his best and was beaten in eight rounds. Boxing hadn't seen the last of him. At the advanced age of 45 he announced a return to the ring. His experience enabled him to win twice in Australia but he was far too old for the hardpunching British champion Scott Welch who broke one of Joe's ribs and rang down the curtain on a career that had begun nearly thirty years earlier.

PRINCE NASEEM HAMED
FEATHERWEIGHT

This unbeaten young man, born in Sheffield but of Yemeni extraction, represents the younger generation of boxing stars. Brash, flashy and supremely confident in his ability to beat the very best, he has risen to world-championship heights without ever being seriously extended. His title win over Steve Robinson was achieved almost effortlessly and, with youth on his side, this charismatic fighter looks like going on and on with many more titles to grace his record before he calls it a day.

Hamed is a product of the Brendan Ingle stable of fighters where a man of similar style – Herol Graham – first came into prominence. Brendan Ingle is not alone in his opinion that Hamed can go on to become the best fighter to come out of Britain since the end of the war.

Naseem began his career in 1992 and only Peter Buckley took him the distance that year. The others lasted, on average, two rounds. This trend continued on to 1994 when European bantamweight champion Vincenzo Belcastro rather unwisely journeyed to Sheffield to put his title on the line against the unbeaten local hero. Belcastro lost every round and barely landed a decent punch on his elusive foe.

With only twelve fights to his record, Hamed set his sights on the world titles

and please note that 'titles' is plural. He defended his new crown against Antonio Picardi and then took on world-rated Freddie Cruz, a veteran with years of boxing behind him. Cruz had never been stopped but after six rounds he had to be rescued by the referee. "I've been in with the best but couldn't do a thing with Hamed", wailed Cruz, and every opponent since then has been frustrated by the superb defensive skills of this young Sheffield Blade.

That game Welsh warrior, Steve Robinson, lasted

eight rounds against Hamed in September of 1995 but when the referee stepped in to save him from further punishment, Robinson had lost not only the fight but his WBO featherweight title. In twenty fights and three years, Naseem Hamed was world champion!

An injury, sustained in training to his right hand, sidelined Hamed until March the following year. To test the strength of the repair he took on fellow southpaw Said Lawal in Glasgow and beat him with

Left : Outstanding talent justifies the confident manner and means that the "Prince" is rarely extended.

just three punches – all from his suspect hand.

Hamed then defended his title against four top-rated men. Daniel Alicia put him down briefly but Naseem rose to take his man apart in the next round. He fought Manuel Medina when suffering with a heavy cold and withstood his challenger's best punches before turning on the heat and stopping him in the eleventh round. Remigio Molina failed to get past the second round.

The test came when IBF king Tom Johnson put his title on the line. Although Johnson was acclaimed as being the best at his weight in the world, Hamed stopped him, and then beat Kevin Kelley by an exciting knockout. Wins over Wayne McCullough and Paul Ingle followed, and Hamed now awaits his next challenger.

AUSTRALIAN STARS

Australia has produced many fine boxers over the past one hundred years, but never, until recently, any fighters who have dominated a weight division at the highest level or who have made a real and lasting impact on the world boxing scene. In the past decade two bright stars – Fenech and Harding – did emerge on to the world stage, and their success may point the way to the future.

As well as the men specially featured below, any round-up of Australian greats would be incomplete without mentioning two other Australian world title winners, Lionel Rose and Jimmy Carruthers, and Peter Jackson, a fine Puerto Rico-born black boxer at the turn of the century who was denied a world title only by the colour bar. Other local heroes who never quite made it to world fame include Les Darcy, Jack Carroll, Ambrose Palmer, Fred Henneberry (who had a long and bitter rivalry with another exceptional Australian middleweight, Ron Richards), Billy Grime, Vic Patrick, and Dave Sands.

Left: Ron Richards, who took on the renowned Fred Henneberry ten times.

FRANK SLAVIN
HEAVYWEIGHT

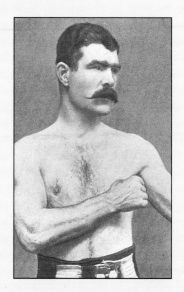

Slavin was born of Irish parents in Maitland, New South Wales, on January 26 1862. Like Bob Fitzsimmons, he worked for a blacksmith in his youth, and developed an impressive and muscular frame: he later went on to find adventure as a gold prospector. He was twenty-three when he fought his first bout, winning a purse of fifty pounds by knocking out Martin Powers.

When the Irishman Jack Burke arrived in Australia in 1889, Slavin was a seasoned professional, and he beat his man in eight rounds. Sensing riches on the world scene, he sailed for England, where he drew with the renowned Jem Smith in a championship contest held at Bruges, Belgium. The championship of England was at stake, and Slavin was having the best of the contest when the fight was deliberately broken up by a gang of toughs who were wearing knuckledusters, who wanted to protect their bets on Smith. Slavin was later awarded the fight, the purse, and the championship title.

He then sailed on to America, where he started his visit with a famous fight against Jake Kilrain, which Slavin won in nine rounds.

While in the United States he sparred with Charlie Mitchell and Jim Daly.

The most significant challenge in the later part of his career came on May 30 1892, against the legendary Peter Jackson, at the National Sporting Club, London, for the title of champion of England and Australia. Slavin was knocked out in the tenth.

In a long and distinguished career, Frank Slavin fought most of the greats of his era, including Smith, Jackson, Jake Kilrain, Joe McAuliffe, Jim Hall and Jack Burke. During a period when the 'world' title was never officially reconciled, he could with some justification lay claim to being the best boxer of his age. He fought on with decreasing frequency until 1907, and died in Canada, in 1929.

'YOUNG GRIFFO'
FEATHERWEIGHT

Right: 'Young Griffo' – Albert Griffiths – (left) takes up a publicity pose against Walter Campbell.

Left: The redoubtable Frank Slavin.

Albert Griffiths was born at Miller's Point, Sydney, in 1871. He started work as a newspaper boy, until a series of successes in street fights tempted him to try his hand as a professional boxer. In modern terms, Griffiths was a feather-weight, but in that period of the fight game's history such subtle distinctions were seldom respected, so 'Young Griffo' made his name by taking on all-comers of many shapes and sizes. His most famous ear-ly encounters came in a series of five bouts against a black boxer from Mel-bourne called Pluto: they drew each contest, the longest being over seventy rounds.

Griffo's first big success came when, weighing only 112 pounds himself, he won a contest for 140 pound boxers: having won national recognition, he proceeded to best all the competition available in his homeland (including Billy Murphy, the darling of the local crowds, on two occa-sions) before setting sail for America to try for world fame and bigger prizes.

In the United States he immediately showed his class by getting the better of draws with three truly excel-lent fighters: Solly Smith, Johnny Van Herst and George Lavigne. He came to be recognized as a ring marvel, and boxing his-torians compare Griffo to one of the all-time greats in the featherweight div-ision, Abe Attell.

He was never a title hol-der, but must be regarded as one of the finest boxers never to wear a crown. He is a legend in the land of his birth, still recognized as one of the earliest and greatest of Australia's sporting heroes.

LES DARCY
MIDDLEWEIGHT

The name of Les Darcy is often overlooked by those who compile lists of all-time great fighters. This is a shocking omission because the young Australian had beaten the best men at his weight when he was in his teens and these were tough, mature fighters who represented a serious threat to any defending champion. Had Darcy's life not ended so tragically and at so young an age, it is indisputable that his name would have been at the very top of the lists.

It seems unimaginable that a nineteen-year-old scrapper could beat the best of American opposition and yet could be the object of deaf ears when title claims were presented. Yet Darcy was. He was one of the strongest middleweight fighters ever. He was bull-necked, muscular, well disciplined, sturdy and a very, very quick learner. He licked Jimmy Clabby, Eddie McGoorty, George Chip and Buck Crouse before his twentieth birthday. Furthermore, McGoorty, Chip and Crouse were stopped inside the distance, and the feared American Jeff Smith looked like going the same way before he fouled out in the second round.

McGoorty, Smith and Jimmy Clabby were formidable men indeed but each one fell at the Les Darcy hurdle. The athleticism of Darcy was apparent right from his schooldays and, with an elder brother being a boxer, Les's path through life was clearly set out. He won several tournaments as a teenager and entered the professional ring at sixteen. He was a natural middleweight, and with plenty of hard manual work to do around his parents' farm, he was in good physical shape all his life. On his way up through the ratings, that crafty veteran Fritz Holland twice outpointed him, but by the time their third meeting came in 1915, Les had matured tremendously and Fritz received a rare beating. This was a twenty round contest, and the young Australian, just nineteen, forced the pace throughout and finished fresh and still full of fight.

The Darcy bandwagon rolled on throughout 1916. At world level now, Les chopped them all down and then set his sights on America. He was the breadwinner at home and had a burning desire to financially set up his parents and brothers and knew that the monetary rewards would be greater in the United States. This was at the time when many young men of his age were being sent off to the battle fields of the First World War and much unfair criticism was heaped on Les when he quietly hopped on a ship for America. His mother had pleaded with him not to enlist because the family would never have managed without his financial support. Also, Les had the encouragement of Tex Rickard who was coming to his peak as a fight promoter.

It was one of those minor matters that we tend to ignore that had sown the seeds of Les Darcy's tragic end. He had set out for America with a broken tooth. Left untreated too

Left: Les Darcy.

long, this later caused the onset of septicaemia and once this got into his bloodstream it became critical, then fatal. Les had been in the States for over six months and several proposed fights had fallen through. His savings had depleted and his patience must have worn very thin with all the broken promises and dashed hopes. These factors, coupled with the obviously depressing bouts of homesickness, probably did more to diminish his spirit than did his opponents in the ring. When he went into hospital in those days prior to the use of modern antibiotics, his will had been weakened. He died aged twenty-one and it is fortunate that in recent years much film footage has been unearthed to remind us of the great potential of James Leslie Darcy. He died with so many fighting years ahead of him and they should have been his best years. Who knows what he may have achieved? His greatness was never fully tested. In 1957, he was elected into the Boxing Hall of Fame.

Above: Les Darcy (left) and Eddie McGoorty.

Below: Darcy (right) shown here against Jimmy Clabby. Les twice outpointed the talented American.

JOHNNY FAMECHON
FEATHERWEIGHT

In the middle years of the twentieth century one of the most noted Australian ring characters was Johnny Famechon. He was born into a great French boxing family (his uncle, Ray, fought for the world championship under the French national colours), but moved to Australia as a child, and began his boxing career in Melbourne in 1961. During the early 1960s he fought only in Melbourne, working his way up through the ranks, until he finally took the Australian featherweight title in his twenty-second professional bout, by beating Ollie Taylor on September 24 1965. Ranging a little further afield – to New South Wales, Queensland, and even Christchurch – he continued to fight regularly and to defend his title, but he always preferred to box in Melbourne whenever possible. It was there, in front of an adoring home crowd, that he advanced his career on November 24 1967 by taking the British Empire crown from Johnny O'Brien. It was not until the following year, 1968, that Famechon fought outside of Australasia for the first time: his fifty-first fight as a professional was held in Paris, against Réné Roque.

Famechon got his shot at the WBC world featherweight title on January 21 1969 in London, and he took the crown by defeating José Legra on points after the full fifteen rounds. He defended the title successfully on two occasions, both fights against 'Fighting' Harada, before being bested by the great Vincente Saldivar on May 9 1970 in Rome. At the age of twenty-five he decided to hang up the gloves, drawing a line under a distinguished career in which he suffered only five defeats in sixty-eight contests.

JEFF FENECH
BANTAMWEIGHT/FEATHERWEIGHT

Fenech was born in Sydney in 1964. Turning professional in 1984, he shot into the limelight by taking a world championship – the IBF bantamweight title – in only his seventh bout, when he defeated Shitoshi Shingaki on April 26 1985.

He defended his new crown three times, including a rematch with Shitoshi, before relinquishing it after a victory on July 18 1986 against Steve McCrory in order to move up to light-featherweight. Less than a year later he was WBC champion in that division after a fourth-round win over Samart Payakarun of Thailand. Again, he defended only twice before giving up the title to move up and fight the featherweights.

On March 7 1988 Fenech met Victor Callejas in Sydney for the WBC featherweight championship, and beat him when the referee stopped the contest in the tenth round. In an extraordinary period of only four years, he had remained unbeaten and taken world titles at three different weights.

Perhaps the most amazing thing about Fenech was that this early success came when he was still a raw fighter with an unrefined technique and an obvious lack of experience: he learnt his trade on the job, and got better every time he entered the ring. One of the highlights of his career was his emphatic victory over Marcus Villasana, which turned into a superb exhibition of ring mastery. Another was a hard-fought fight against Azumah Nelson, in which Nelson was lucky to escape with a draw; although an eventual defeat by the same boxer in March 1992 represented a major set-back. Nevertheless Fenech, by virtue of holding three titles and of gaining world recognition for Australian boxing, lays claim to being the greatest of all the products of the Australian fight game: he is revered as a national hero.

Top left: Johnny Famechon (left) misses with a left in a non-title encounter with a young Miguel Herrera.

Right: Jeff Fenech, arguably Australia's finest boxer ever. He commenced a comeback campaign in 1995 and fought successfully enough to secure a rematch with Nelson.

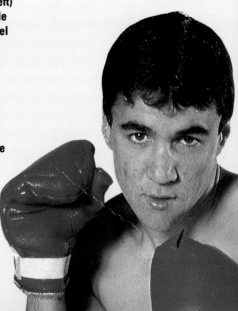

JEFF HARDING
LIGHT-HEAVYWEIGHT

Left: Jeff Harding, looking formidably aggressive even between rounds.

Although Fenech may have put together the more impressive track record, there is no doubt that 'Hit Man' Harding produced the greatest ever night for Australian boxing when, in June 1989, he came from nowhere (as a late substitute for Donny Lalonde) to beat the established world light-heavyweight champion, Dennis Andries, and take the title.

Came from nowhere, that is, according to the American and British critics: the home commentators had seen enough of Harding's toughness, fitness, and firepower during the first seven years of his career to know that an upset was on the cards. Andries, too, was taken by surprise, and later admitted that he had failed to do his homework on the relative unknown. The result was that, after his normal strong start, showing his experience and highlighting the Australian's weaknesses, Andries gradually found himself going further and further backwards, until, to the astonishment and delight of the New Jersey crowd (who knew they were witnessing the start of something special), Harding stopped him for good after one minute twenty-five seconds of the twelfth round.

The highs and lows of Harding's career have all come against Andries. His first professional defeat came in their rematch, when the challenger, better prepared now he realised what he was up against, came through strongly to recover his title. Then Harding, proving to be one of the most determined and bloody-minded boxers in history, bested Andries in their third encounter to recapture the crown.

Harding's grittiest performance followed a period of inactivity. In 1994 he opposed the craftsman Mike McCallum. It was experience beating youth and the veteran Jamaican took Jeff's title. However, there was warm praise for Harding from McCallum for having given him his hardest fight.

INDEX

Ali, Muhammad 82, 92–3, 94, 95, 96, 98, 120 *see also* Clay, Cassius
Armstrong, Henry 54–5
Attell, Abe 36, 37, 123

Baer, Max 52–3, 60
Basilio, Carmen 70, 71, 81
Bassey, Hogan 'Kid' 78
Beckett, Joe 35, 40
Belcher, John 'Jem' 14, 16
Benitez, Wilfred 101, 104
Benn, Nigel 116
Berbick, Trevor 93, 112
Bowe, Riddick 114
Braddock, James J. 53, 60
Britton, Jack 42–3, 48
Broughton, Jack 11–12
Bruno, Frank 112, 115, 120
Bugner, Joe 94, 120
Burke, James 'Deaf 'Un' 17–19
Burns, Tommy 32, 34–5
Byrne, Simon 16, 17

Carnera, Primo 52, 60
Carpentier, Georges 40–1, 43, 44, 46
Caunt, Ben 18, 19
Cerdan, Marcel 56, 62–3, 76–7
Charles, Ezzard 58, 59, 60, 72–3
Chavez, Julio Cesar 109, 110–11
Choynski, Julio Cesar 30, 31
Clay, Cassius 90 *see also* Ali, Muhammad
Conn, Billy 56, 59
Conteh, John 119
Cooney, Gerry 97, 98, 99
Cooper, Henry 88, 90–1, 92, 120
Corbett, James J. 22, 23, 26, 28–9, 30–1
Creedon, Dan 28, 29
Cribb, Thomas 14, 15, 16, 20

Darcy, Les 124–5
De La Hoya, Oscar 109, 111
Dempsey, Jack 40, 41, 44–5, 46, 53, 68, 74
Douglas, James 'Buster' 112
Downes, Terry 118
Driscoll, Jim 36–7
Duran, Roberto 100–1, 102, 103, 104
Durelle, Yvon 64, 65

Eubank, Chris 116

Famechon, Johnny 126
Farr, Tommy 53, 60
Fenech, Jeff 108, 122, 126
Figg, James 11
Fitzsimmons, Bob 28–9, 30, 31
Flowers, Tiger 48
Flynn, Jim 32, 34, 39
Foreman, George 58, 93, 94, 96–7, 98
Frazier, Joe 93, 94–5, 96, 97, 98, 120
Fullmer, Gene 70

Golota, Andrew 114, 115
Graziano, Rocky 56, 57, 70, 74–5, 100
Greb, Harry 46, 48
Griffiths, Albert 'Young Griffo' 123
Gully, John 14–16

Hagler, Marvin 101, 102–3, 104
Hamed, Prince Naseem 121
Harding, Jeff 122, 127
Hearns, Thomas 101, 104, 105
Heenan, John C. 20, 21, 23
Holmes, Larry 93, 94, 98–9, 112
Holyfield, Evander 97, 98, 112, 114, 115

Jackson, 'Gentleman' John 13–14
Jackson, Peter 22, 23, 30, 122
Jeanette, Joe 38, 39
Johansson, Ingemar 88–9, 90
Johnson, Jack 25, 32–3, 35, 38–9, 40
Jones, Roy 117
Kane, Peter 66–7

Kearns, Jack 'Doc' 44, 49, 64
Ketchel, Stanley 32, 33
Kilrain, Jake 26, 27, 122

LaMotta, Jake 62, 70, 76–7, 100
Langan, Jack 16
Langford, Sam 38–9
Ledoux, Charles 36, 37
Leonard, 'Sugar' Ray 100, 103, 104–5
Lesnevich, Gus 68, 72
Levinsky, 'Battling' 40, 46
Lewis, Lennox 114, 115
Lewis, Ted 'Kid' 40, 42–3
Liston, Sonny 89, 92, 93
Loughran, Tommy 48, 49, 53
Louis, Joe 50, 51, 52, 53, 58, 59, 60–1, 70, 72, 73, 80, 82
Lyle, Ron 96–7
Lynch, Benny 66

Mace, 'Jem' 22, 23, 28
Marciano, Rocky 58, 59, 61, 65, 73, 82–3, 113
Mauriello, Tami 59
Maxim, Joey 64, 68, 69, 70, 72
McCall, Oliver 98, 115
McGuigan, Barry 106–7, 119
McVey, Sam 38, 39
Mendoza, Daniel 12–13, 30
Mills, Freddie 68–9
Mitchell, Charlie 26, 27, 30
Molineaux, Tom 14, 15, 16, 20
Moore, Archie 64–5
Moore, Davey 101
Moorer, Michael 97

Nelson, Azumah 108, 109, 126
Norton, Ken 93, 96, 98

O'Brien, Jack 'Philadelphia' 29, 34
Olson, 'Bobo' 70, 71, 86

Paddock, James 19, 20
Patterson, Floyd 64, 88, 89, 112
Pearce, Henry 'Game Chicken' 14, 15
Pender, Paul 70, 118
Pep, Willie 78–9, 84

Rickard, Tex 40, 41, 44, 47, 124
Robinson, 'Sugar' Ray 62, 70–1, 74, 76, 77, 78, 81, 86, 87, 118
Ruddock, Donovan 'Razor' 115
Ryan, Paddy 23, 26, 27

Saddler, Sandy 78, 79, 84–5
Sayers, Tom 20, 21, 22, 23
Schmeling, Max 48, 49, 50–1, 52, 60, 61
Sharkey, Jack 45, 48, 49, 50
Slack, Jack 11–12, 14
Slavin, Frank 122
Smith, James 'Bonecrusher' 98, 112
Spinks, Michael 98, 112
Sullivan, John L. 22, 23, 26–7, 29, 30, 74

Thompson, William 'Bendigo' 18, 19
Tunney, Gene 40, 44, 46–7, 50
Turpin, Randolph 70, 86–7
Tyson, Mike 24, 94, 98, 99, 112–13, 115

Walcott, Jersey Joe 58–9, 60, 61, 72–3, 82, 83
Walker, Mickey 48–9, 50, 51
Ward, James 'Jem' 16–17
Watson, Michael 116
Welsh, Freddie 36, 37
Willard, Jess 25, 32, 44, 45
Williams, Ike 80–1
Wills, Harry 38, 39
Wright, Chalky 78, 79

Zale, Tony 56–7, 63, 74, 75